To Dusty and His Mother

KEN LOEFFLER ON BASKETBALL

KEN LOEFFLER

ON

BASKETBALL

by
KEN LOEFFLER
with
RALPH BERNSTEIN

PRENTICE-HALL, INC.

ENGLEWOOD CLIFFS, N. J.

PRINTED IN THE UNITED STATES OF AMERICA

51481

Grateful acknowledgment is made to Brother David, Public Relations Director of LaSalle College, for his help in preparing the illustrations for this book.

CONTENTS

PUBLISHER'S FOREWORD

KEN LOEFFLER HAS REMARKED IN JEST ON MANY occasions that he would never write a book, for then everyone would be as smart as he is. If that sounds brash and boastful it is not meant to be. But rather it is Loeffler's way of constantly and consistently stating what he believes to be the truth, regardless of the consequences. He could never be classified as a wallflower, a shy, retiring, blushing gentleman of modest or falsely modest manner.

Writer, law professor, raconteur, telecaster, musician. He plays the piano, saxophone, and uke. Writer, poet and basketball coach, Loeffler is a man of many talents. In the language of the press, he is colorful, controversial, humorous, and a master of the game he teaches—basketball. When he is referred to

1

as "controversial," Loeffler generally will reply that "if speaking the truth makes me controversial, then I am that, because truth is so rarely heard in this world of mice."

It's a toss-up as to whether Loeffler is best known for the fine basketball teams he has produced, in both the collegiate and professional ranks, or for his ability to create controversy at the sound of a basketball whistle. He probably has become involved in more rhubarbs than the redoubtable Kansas Cyclone, Phog Allen. And once he latches on to a good argument Loeffler rarely lets go of it without having the last word, or the "last good word," as he puts it.

There was the night back in 1951 when Loeffler took his highly rated LaSalle team to Raleigh, North Carolina for a game with North Carolina State. North Carolina State won 76–74, but the game itself was dwarfed by the roar that went up from the LaSalle dressing room after it was all over. Loeffler, as you will see in the pages to follow, never hesitates to speak his mind, not even in the lion's den—or in this case the Wolfpack's Lair. He felt his team had been done in by the officials and he said so. "This," said Loeffler, referring to the game, "is the biggest steal since the Louisiana Purchase."

The battle of words among Loeffler, the officials, and North Carolina State Coach Everett Case made newspaper headlines for several days. Then, as all controversies do, the story died. But not with Loeffler.

The following summer he and Case were flying across the Atlantic together to teach in a basketball clinic in Germany. The passengers were informed that the plane was unable to land at Keflavik, Iceland, and would have to proceed to Scotland. Case was sleeping. Suddenly, Loeffler shook him violently. "Everett, we can't land at Keflavik. We're going on to Scotland and may not make it. Quick, before we go down, admit those officials at Raleigh were terrible."

What kind of man is Ken Loeffler, many people ask. Well, one person who knows him well once said, "Personally, I admire the man as a master of basketball technique and as a handler of boys, as well as for his very modern approach to the game. However, I wonder about his egotistical attitude, the manner in which he sometimes pops off, and his apparently consuming ambition for the limelight. There is no doubt that he is one of the most interesting men in sports I have ever met."

Frankly, Loeffler willingly accepts that description of him. But he believes that his attitude is not one of ego, but rather one of confidence: a veneer of assurance he wants to transfer to his players. He believes that when he speaks his mind he is not popping off, but merely expressing his honest opinion of a given situation. And he believes that he has *no* consuming ambition for the limelight, but that he is human and enjoys the glory that surrounds his success. Loeffler says, "Coaching is no popularity contest. I've been criticized for sounding off, but I've never said anything I didn't believe."

And the boys who have played for him, the students he has taught in the classrooms, will tell you that this straightforward manner makes Loeffler an ideal coach and teacher. They'll tell you that they always know where they stand. He has shown his players that there is much more to the game of basketball than a ball and two baskets. Loeffler treats the game like a chess match. He believes firmly that in most cases personnel are virtually equal, and that the team that makes the more intelligent moves will win.

In practice sessions he constantly stresses the difference between what he calls intelligent mistakes and wild mistakes. An intelligent mistake, Loeffler says, is an error of commission in which a player makes the right move but fails to carry it out because of some unforeseen circumstance. This type of mistake he forgives. But a wild mistake, he asserts, is an attempt to do something the player never should have tried in the first place, even if it works. This type of error draws his ire.

Loeffler's sharp tongue and quick wit are ever in evidence. Several years ago he took his LaSalle team into the mecca of college basketball, Madison Square Garden in New York. In order to overcome a deficiency in height, he ordered his team into a zone defense. This slowed down the game. The spectators stamped their feet and booed. After the game the New York basketball writers roasted the LaSalle coach unmercifully in their columns.

Loeffler read and remembered. Almost a year later he once again brought his team to New York. He told a sportswriter during an interview that he might use the zone defense again, if he could get the permission of the New York writers. During a time-out he called the officials over and, just to rub it in, told them to ask the writers at the press table if it was okay for LaSalle to use a zone. Ken was jesting, but the incident is indicative of his entire outlook. He had to have the last "good" word.

During his six years at LaSalle, Loeffler's teams won 145 games and lost only 30, and played in a post-season tournament every year, winning the National Invitational Championship in 1952, the National Collegiate Athletic Association title in 1954, and finishing runner-up in the 1955 NCAA tourney. His LaSalle teams established an NCAA record of nine straight tournament victories before losing in NCAA competition. Hank Iba's Oklahoma Aggie teams held the old mark of eight straight wins before suffering an NCAA defeat. In addition to his fine teams, Loeffler has the distinction of having developed a boy described by most basketball experts as the greatest all-around player of all time—Tom Gola.

Somehow, Loeffler's most notable debates seem to result from games with North Carolina State. The story of "The Letter" certainly bears repeating in any profile on Ken Loeffler. The letter was written by

Loeffler to Referee Phil Fox before the LaSalle–North Carolina State game of 1955. It wasn't disclosed until after the contest at Raleigh, from which State emerged a slim winner. Fox revealed that Loeffler had written him a letter which the referee threatened to turn over to the Federal Bureau of Investigation. Fox claimed that the coach had attempted to intimidate him and that he considered the letter unethical.

Loeffler wasn't the least bit taken aback by Fox's statements and implications. He commented that there was nothing nasty in the letter and that, as usual, he had merely expressed his beliefs to the referee. Loeffler told Fox he personally objected to him as an official. He explained that Fox's work the previous year in a LaSalle–North Carolina State game had not been satisfactory. He wrote further, "I felt also that you definitely leaned toward North Carolina State in your calls, and was determined at the time that, if I had anything to do with it, you would never officiate for us again.

"Now I find that, in spite of my objections to your officiating, you will work our game Saturday night. . . . . You must gather by this time that I am completely unhappy about the situation, over which I have no control.

"However, we are having motion pictures taken of the game and will have foul calls photographed, with the idea that I will use them in my coaching schools this summer and in other demonstrations."

Fox eventually dropped the whole matter. And Loeffler, in his honest manner, said he had no complaint about Fox's work in the game. "Fox called a satisfactory game," he said. "Maybe I'll use those films we took and show how well he worked."

Now why would a coach write such a letter to an official? Loeffler wasn't trying to intimidate Fox. He merely saw a situation that he believed might hurt the chances of his boys' winning a game. As their coach he took a step he thought necessary to protect their interests. He felt he wouldn't deserve to be a coach if he didn't button up all the angles in preparing for a game. And Loeffler is a coach who looks in all corners for possible booby traps. Maybe he was wrong. Maybe he shouldn't have written the letter. But Loeffler believed it was right. That was enough for him. He remarked later that this was the first such letter he had written to an official in 25 years of coaching, in itself a compliment to officials.

Loeffler's career has been varied. He has coached football, baseball, and basketball. And his basketball coaching spans the Ivy League, the pros, and LaSalle—a top independent. Now he's headed for the wide-open spaces of Texas to try to lead the Texas A. & M. cadets out of the basketball wilderness.

He says of his pro days that it was like crowding fifteen years of coaching into three years.

"I've been asked why I left the pros," he has said, "especially St. Louis, where we won the division crown one year. Well, there were two contributing factors. One was the terrific toll the pro game takes on your health, and the other was Jim Pollard."

It's easy to understand the health problem. Coaching pro basketball is a tough job—the headaches and heartaches, along with the incessant traveling. New York's Joe Lapchick collapsed one year. One pro coach jokingly said he was afraid to go into tall buildings after his team had lost thirteen straight—afraid he might jump. The Warriors' Eddie Gottlieb developed gall bladder trouble. But what's this business about Pollard?

Loeffler says that when he first took over the St. Louis Bombers, the one player he wanted on his team was Jim Pollard. He thought Pollard was the best basketball player he'd ever seen, better than George Mikan, Joe Fulks, and Hank Luisetti. So he got together with Pollard's agent, who said Jim would play for Loeffler for $12,000. Loeffler talked it over with the team's accountant and the salary was okayed. Loeffler then wrote to Pollard, but "Big Jim" never answered. He wound up with the Minneapolis Lakers. Two years later Loeffler asked Pollard why he had never answered his letter. Pollard said, "What letter?" It seems the St. Louis accountant had got to thinking that $12,000 for one basketball player was too much and had never sent the letter.

Loeffler was born in Beaver Falls, Pa. His adolescent ambition was to become a lawyer. He graduated from Penn State, where he played basketball and baseball and messed around with boxing and wrestling.

He later played professional basketball in Pittsburgh for four years.

His call as a coach came in 1928, four years after he left State. Geneva College in his home town of Beaver Falls wanted Loeffler as their basketball coach. He accepted and decided to attend the University of Pittsburgh Law School at the same time. Upon graduating from law school in 1934, Loeffler took an examination to qualify for the Federal Bureau of Investigation. He passed. But before he ever got to Washington, an offer came from Yale University to coach basketball at the famed New Haven institution. Loeffler couldn't resist a coaching offer, especially one from a university like Yale, so the FBI lost an agent and basketball retained a fine coach.

Yale didn't provide Ken with too many spare moments. In addition to coaching basketball, he served as assistant baseball coach and assistant football coach. It was while at Yale that Loeffler met a nurse named Helen Whitman from the New Haven Hospital. She became Mrs. Ken Loeffler in August, 1938.

Ken finally left the hallowed halls of old Eli in 1942, to join the Army Air Corps. He always likes to refer to his Yale days as a pleasant period of molding character, since the university, minus top-flight material, didn't cut much of a figure in basketball circles. The court game was considered a minor sport at that time. Loeffler says he held his job and the goodwill of the brethren down at Mori's by beating Harvard and Princeton sufficiently in Big Three games.

Loeffler was a major when discharged from the Air Corps in 1945. He had served as a member of many court martial boards and was commanding officer of several Air Corps training detachments. One was a pre-flight unit at Butler University, and another a school for making flight teachers of former fliers at Spartan Air Craft, Tulsa, Oklahoma. He completed his service in the office of the Assistant Chief of the Air Staff with headquarters in the Pentagon, Washington, D. C.

After leaving the service, Loeffler filled in for a year at Denver University as an assistant football and basketball coach for the regular coach, who was still in the service. From there he went to the professional league. He was on a dude ranch he operated in the summer months when the call came offering him the job as coach of the St. Louis Bombers in the Basketball Association of America.

When he wasn't running the dude ranch in Wyoming, Loeffler worked for the New York Yankees in their baseball try-out system. On his ranch he suffered a back injury while trying to break a horse. The injury has left him with a numb left leg. This, together with a bad knee and a nearly fatal attack of bleeding ulcers, hepatitis from blood transfusions, pneumonia, and phlebitis, have kept him physically miserable, but highly philosophical. He says he'd rather die on the bench than in a hospital bed, adding that he hopes one of his players of Gola's stature has the ball with 30 seconds to play and his team leading by three points when he passes out. Then, he says, I could go in peace.

In 1954, with his bottle of milk and blue ulcer pills resting alongside the bench, Loeffler directed his team to the finals of the NCAA tournament, where it finally was defeated by San Francisco.

Loeffler may not admit this, but his 1953–54 NCAA champions represented his greatest achievement. He expected to have a veteran team for that season, but wound up winning the top prize in collegiate ranks with three sophomores, a junior, and one senior. Ineligibility and the decision of a returning service star to turn professional reduced what should have been an experienced squad to a comparatively green team. Of course, Loeffler had Gola, but even an All-American of Gola's caliber doesn't make a team. Perhaps to the surprise of many, it still takes five men to produce a winning basketball team.

Everyone expected Loeffler to build his team around Gola, and he did, but not exactly in the way they pictured. He didn't make a stationary pivot of big Tom and have the other players concentrate on throwing the ball into the pivot. Loeffler reasoned that Gola, being human, might have a bad night or two. And, when he did, the others had to be ready to take up the slack. So he built a balanced team. Gola was the star, but he didn't specialize in the pivot. Tom developed his skills evenly, as did the others. As a result, Gola developed into the finest all-around performer possible.

LaSalle lost only four games, and at one stage of the season put together an eleven-game winning streak. It went to the NCAA tourney and marched through to the final against Bradley. One of the most pleasing victories for Loeffler was a preliminary round triumph over Everett Case's North Carolina State Wolfpack. In the final, LaSalle treated a capacity crowd in Kansas City to a captivating exhibition of basketball as it walloped Bradley to capture the crown. Most of the credit for the season's record naturally goes to the boys. But it wouldn't be an exaggeration to say they probably wouldn't have made it without the keen, analytical, scientific direction of Ken Loeffler.

The finest tribute to Loeffler's stature as a coach is the constant demand for his services at basketball clinics all over the world. Other coaches, especially high school mentors, want to hear his theories of coaching basketball. They're different, as you will see in this book. Georgia Tech beat Kentucky twice in the 1955 season. But what very few people know is that the Georgia Tech coach, John Hyder, adopted some Loeffler methods to turn the trick, including an almost unheard of win on Kentucky's own court at Lexington. Hyder picked up these tips at one of Ken's clinics.

Loeffler has become quite a traveler. He conducts basketball coaching clinics every summer for the Armed Forces in Europe. He visited Puerto Rico one year to pass along his methods, and recently completed a tour of South and Central America for the State Department.

He taught basketball as part of the Department's campaign to combat Communism with Democracy in Latin America. He took Gola along on this mission, using the All-American as a model in his classes. Loeffler, who took special Spanish lessons for the tour, spoke on basketball, showed motion pictures, and had Gola demonstrate the techniques he teaches to his players.

Additional honors earned by this solid citizen of basketball include his having been named Coach of the Year twice by the Philadelphia Basketball Writers Association and, in 1954–55, his selection to coach the East All-Star team in two post-season games, one at Kansas City and the other in New York. Loeffler's smartly coached all-stars won handily on both occasions. As coach of the East team in the New York game he joined the honor roll of such former East coaches as Joe Lapchick, then of St. John's; Nat Holman, of CCNY; Ben Carnevale, Navy; Adolph Rupp, Kentucky; Dr. Harold Carlson, Pitt; Clair Bee, LIU; Honey Russell, Seton Hall; and Howard Cann, NYU.

Now Loeffler begins a new chapter of his life as he moves to the Southwest, where football has always been king. He has taken over a team at Texas A. & M. which finished last in its conference and won only four games in 1954–55. He has been given the job of making a basketball power of the Aggies. He'll bring a different style of basketball to the area. The expressive Loeffler should prove a match for anything he meets in Texas, whether it be on the basketball court, in the banquet hall, or in the classroom.

If Texas A. & M. is wondering what kind of a coach it is getting, the following little story should be enlightening. LaSalle had won 21 straight games over a two-season period when it lost to Utah at Madison Square Garden in New York. Loeffler walked toward the LaSalle dressing room with Brother David, the college public relations director. "I'm sick and tired of losing," growled Loeffler.

Brother David looked at the coach in amazement. "Why Ken," he said, "this is the first game we've lost in more than a year."

"That's what I mean," replied Loeffler. "I'm sick and tired of losing."

INCENTIVE
BASKETBALL

THERE ARE A HUNDRED DIFFERENT WAYS TO PLAY basketball, many of which are equally successful as long as the ball winds up in the basket at the end of a maneuver. Kentucky under Adolph Rupp plays a style of its own; St. Louis coached by Eddie Hickey has its pattern of play; Henry Iba teaches still another method at Oklahoma A. & M.; Dudie Moore's Duquesne team has its style trademark. Certain ball-handling methods and defensive patterns distinguish these men and their teams from other teams. These differences hold the interest of the players and the fans. Famous coaches now select the types of material that will fit into their pattern of play. But it wasn't always that way.

In the beginning basketball was played to fill the

void between the football and baseball seasons. It was a game to occupy the fans and players until the baseball season opened up again. The fans could gather in a warm auditorium or gymnasium to discuss the batting averages of their hitting heroes and the long runs of their favorite halfbacks. The players could get some good exercise thumping each other. And thump each other they did, with an unlimited number of players on each side. Running with the ball was permitted and there were no fouls for contact. The only object— I guess it's still the only object—was to get the ball into the basket. But some observant gentleman, as is always the case, saw possibilities in the game. He found that if men were properly spaced or deployed around the court they were more successful in keeping the defense spread. And so the first system of offense was born.

Then, because an unlimited number of players made for too much congestion, the teams were cut to seven, then six, and finally to five on a side. The rulemakers found that with six on a side the entire defensive area was overguarded. Can you imagine six-man zone defenses? It's hard enough to get through a five-man zone. But with a five-man team there was an open area for the offense to operate in. Thus the quintet was created. The game became scientific. Brains, not brawn, became the prime requisite of basketball. The watchers did more watching, the players did more maneuvering, and the greatest of all spectator sports was out of the cradle—not only walking, but running and dribbling.

Before getting on with the evolution of the game, I am reminded by a history professor friend of mine that a form of basketball was played by the Inca Indians in the 16th century. The ball was tossed through a circular stone ring, placed on an abutting cliff perpendicular to the ground, rather than parallel as present baskets are. It also seems, the history prof tells me, that for scoring a field goal the player was permitted to select an article of wearing apparel from any fan he desired—a piece of jewelry, a hat, or whatever he wished. So even in that day the professional athlete existed.

We will gloss over the era of the center jump, the standing and running guards, and the forwards who were supposed to do most of the scoring, and enter into the era of modern basketball—where everyone is supposed to score. But somewhere along the line something happened in the form of the "big man" the "big pivot man." No one quite knows exactly when the pivot play started. There are various ideas and we'll submit one which appears to be as logical as any.

Men who stood in the rear court and did nothing but defend were called "standing guards." Their sole job was to guard men dashing down the floor and rebound the defensive board. These standing guards would stand in the area of the defensive foul line and never, or rarely, would venture up the court. Their pride was that they would rarely score a field goal. Then the old New York Celtics' professional basketball team found that one standing guard was giving them a rough time. So "Dutch" Dehnert went down the court and put his back to him to block him away from covering the Celtics. Someone passed "Dutch" the ball and the pivot play was born.

The advent of the Mikans, Kurlands, and other excessively big men brought a new hue to technical basketball. The big man did most of the scoring and the other men performed in supporting cast roles. The other four players became *less* important while the big man became *more* important. The search for the big pivot man became furious. Basketball had lost its balance and the nonpivot men were losing their incentive. No longer could they dash through the middle of the court for layups under the basket.

But what about the teams that had no giant to throw the ball to? They were forced to adopt a movable offense that might compensate for their lack of height. They developed speed to offset this physical disadvantage. And, aided by recent rule changes like the widening of the foul lane, more and more teams are now adopting the balanced non-set pivot attack. The widening of the lane has restricted the movements of the big man in the basket area.

This book then will be devoted to incentive, weave-screen, flash-pivot basketball, as played by teams like LaSalle, winner of 145 out of 175 games in the past six years, including a National Invitation tournament championship, one NCAA title, and one NCAA runner-up finish. The main discussion of offense will be about incentive offense, along with defensive techniques peculiar to our style of play and overall game plans. But why the word "incentive"? Because each man is required to execute every skill: screening, set shooting, flash-pivot play, rebounding. Each man is a balanced performer and, equipped to execute all of the skills of the game, he has a greater *incentive* to master them. He is no longer a supporting actor. He too is a king. He is just as important as the old feature player, the set pivot man.

If there is any social benefit in playing a team game, this balanced attack should make for balanced individuals with balanced viewpoints. Getting along with others is the essence of sportsmanship. It is an attribute that I fear is sadly lacking in this world of ours.

You may ask, how can you play this kind of basketball when everyone else isn't playing it. You have answered your own question. St. Louis won in the old Basketball Association of America without a set pivot man. And other teams all over the country are winning every season the same way—without pivot kings. This moving game puts a different defensive burden on the opposing team that they are not accustomed to coping with. Each defensive man must defend all over the court. The defensive set pivot is forced to run if he wants to properly defend. The analogy can be drawn to a football field, where teams that were accus-

19

tomed to defending against split-T formations are suddenly confronted with a single wing.   The single wing
becomes effective because it is different.

Having sown the seeds of incentive basketball, now
let's talk about the selection of material.

☆ 2

SELECTION OF
MATERIAL

THERE ARE THREE TYPES OF COLLEGES OR UNIVER-
sities to consider in discussing the selection of material.
Let's assume for the sake of analysis that Class One is
the school or college that cannot select but has to make
do with the basketball material in its student body.   It
has no recruitment program.   Class Two would include
institutions that can offer some benefits for their athletes.   And Class Three would be the ones that, because
of their size and resources, can go out and get the material necessary for success.   Recognizing the limita-
tions of the first two classes, we will take for this discussion the third group which can select ideal material.

In the East-West All-Star game at Kansas City in
1955 and in the East-West game in New York, I coached
what I think (and many others thought so too) was an

ideal incentive-material team.   On it were Tom Gola, LaSalle; Maurice Stokes, St. Francis (Loretto, Pa.); Dick Ricketts, Duquesne; Ed Conlin, Fordham; and Corky Devlin, George Washington.   All were six feet, five inches tall or better, had their shoulders set fairly high, could move (give-and-go and screen), could play the moving pivot, and, above all, could defend.   Most of them had played man-for-man tag defense during their collegiate careers.   We had the real *Incentive Basketball Team* on the court and the results of the games proved their talents and the merits of the system.

I am often asked by older fans and players, "What happened to the little man in basketball?"   A friend of mine answered that question: "He's refereeing."   This is not meant to be a slap at the little man.   There are some great ones in the game, but they will be the first to tell you how much they suffer, particularly in defense.

Let's define the types of players before we go into a more detailed discussion of their desirable qualities. We'll call the little men those up to six feet, two inches; the medium-sized men those from six feet, three to six feet, seven inches; and the big men those over six feet, eight inches.   There are plenty of six foot-two men to go around, but the competition for the other two groups is brutal.   The six-foot-two-inch man must be a great outside shot for the obvious reason that, if he goes inside, the larger defensive man will block his close shots. The six-foot-ten-inch man largely plays inside so he can do rebound work.   He plays inside also because he generally is unable to move as fast as men in the other two groups. It is a significant thing, and a frightening one also, that the two most publicized players of the 1955 season were approximately seven feet tall: namely Wilt ("The Stilt") Chamberlain, a fine Philadelphia high school player, and Bill Russell of San Francisco University's national champions.

Unless rule-makers make some adjustments forbidding certain offensive maneuvers to the seven-foot man, the game will be reduced to a travesty. But more of that later in Chapter 12.

Hewing to our theme then of selecting material for the incentive basketball system, it would seem we should look for the middle group player, the six-foot-six-inch boy who can move fairly well for screening purposes, can shoot well behind a moving screen, and is big enough and agile enough to do both defensive and offensive rebounding. Such material existed on the East College All-Star Team in 1955, and I really believe that team could have gone on to win the national professional basketball championship if it had been handled properly and had used a balanced screen weave, set shot, and flash-pivot offense. They played balanced incentive basketball at its best.

What happens to the little man and the big, slow man? They too have a place in the basketball picture, but in a different style of attack, in a style not so effective as the one we're advocating. They are the boys who will play in the more or less set pivot-play systems.

In the rear court these systems have two feeders who must be good set shots and passers, and in the corners two good rebounders to help the big, slow man working the set pivot attack near the basket.

In addition to the three height groups, our next classifications are based on speed. Basketball is a game of speed—speed in passing, speed in driving, speed all over the court. Speed and size join hands in the ideal material selection search. They are the two things a coach can't develop. There are many successful basketball players who do not have real speed; but they have a quickness in their first step and an overall agility that compensates to some extent for their lack of real speed.

It is heart breaking to get letters from fond parents with sons six feet tall and no speed who have been fair high school players. The parents have dreams of their boys playing top college basketball. There are untold thousands of boys who will never make it because they lack one of the three distinctive elements necessary to make up a prime college prospect: namely, (1) extreme size, (2) extreme mobility, and (3) extreme shooting ability. If you can't qualify in at least two or all of these three elements, your chances of basketball success at the top collegiate level are poor.

It might be well to mention here that college coaches are having great difficulty in evaluating prospective material because of the increased use of the zone defense at the high school level. In the zone boys are not forced to move and react so quickly as they have to in man-for-man defense. Thus coaches are limited in judging their real worth.

Once you have established that a boy has the physical attributes you want, the next step is to talk to the parents, the high school principal, and the coach. The average high school coach can tell you more about a boy than the parents. It has been my experience that, if you tell the high school coach the type of youngster you're looking for, he'll usually give you the player you want. Naturally, you should check a boy's grades in order to be sure he is college material scholastically. A boy who becomes ineligible because of scholastic deficiency is no good to the team. In all fairness, however, many athletes, who later became good students, had been permitted to drift through high school and didn't have to acquire good study habits until they arrived in college.

We assume the boy has enough pride to keep himself in physical condition. Anyone who doesn't stay in shape is wasting his time and the coach's also. There you have it—the boy we want for our incentive basketball: the six-foot-six-inch 190-pounder with good grades, speed, desire, and pride.

Now let's take a look at the boy's side of the picture in his selection of a college. The sensible way to go about it is for the coach to sit down with the boy and the parents and learn what the boy wants to study and plans to do after he graduates from college. What course is he interested in taking in college? Where does he want to live after he has finished school? Does he want to go on to graduate school? Will his parents be able to give him financial aid when he gets to college? These and many others are questions that should be talked over with the boy and his parents to prevent future misunderstandings and unhappiness on both sides.

Peck Hickman, the very able coach of Louisville University, tells the story of the boy he talked to about attending Louisville. Peck seemed unable to get to the boy and find out his thoughts. "Isn't there someone you want to be proud of you?" he asked. No reaction.

"Don't you have a mother or sweetheart whom you would like to please by getting an education and by being written about in the sports sections?" No reaction.

"Tell me, son, isn't there *something* you'd rather do more than anything in the world?"

Suddenly the boy's eyes lit up. He looked out the window at a man on a motorcycle and said, "Yes, coach, there is; if I could just get me one of them things and ride it!"

Much has been said about modern youth and its careless attitude and unwillingness to accept responsibility. That to me in most instances is a completely unfair and isolated evaluation of the modern young collegian. First, if he is that way his predecessors had something to do with it by being phonies themselves. My observation of most prospective athletes, is that they're not buncoed by their elders. So my approach to a boy going to college and becoming a student and basketball player is a completely honest and frontal one. The college has certain things to offer the boy in the way of education and aid. The boy has latent ability to offer the team, which in turn ensures his overall education and development. Winning is important too —at least winning enough to know the feeling of a job well done. But winning isn't the only end. This chapter probably should be called "Selection of the Boy and the College"—a mutual agreement reached without high-pressure methods.

Such an arrangement has more lasting qualities.

INDIVIDUAL
OFFENSIVE
SKILLS

THE STORY IS TOLD OF A HIGH SCHOOL CHEMISTRY professor who was appointed by his principal to coach the basketball team. Knowing nothing about the technique of the game, he faced up the problem in his first meeting with the squad by pointing to the baskets and saying, "Boys, the object of this game is to get the ball into the basket." How true this is.

SHOOTING

Teams, mine included, can pass, dribble, finesse,

fake, and execute all the fine skills with perfection; but unless they get the ball in the basket all goes for naught. The first approach then, putting first things first, should be a discussion of the technique of shooting. No attempt will be made to discuss the fundamentals of every shot, but rather shooting as it relates to the basketball pattern we advocate.

And also, before getting into this phase of basketball, let's look at basketball shooting from the standpoint of "when to shoot and when not to."

One of the marks of a finished basketball performer is that he never takes any bad shots—shots from bad positions, hurried shots, shots when no teammate is in position for rebounding. Coaching patterns largely determine when and where shots should be taken. Some patterns (Oklahoma A. & M.) stress ball control and encourage a minimum of shooting. Some patterns (the old Rhode Island State and the pro teams) encourage a maximum of shooting. In between these two styles lies the field of balanced attack—balance between passing, moving, and shooting, balance between offense and defense—that we will stress throughout this book.

The perfect basketball player should have a variety of shots. Most commonly used are the two-handed set, the jump shot, the stab, the underhand layup and the turn hook shot, although the turn hook has been replaced in part by the effective pivot jump turn shot. These are the standard basic shots. We'll discuss them in relation to the development of the balanced player in our incentive basketball pattern.

The ball should be carried in what is called the triple-threat position. Shooting should be tied in with the threat of a dribble drive so that the offensive man can get enough space to shoot *without a set screen* in front of him. The triple-threat position is just what its name sounds like. A football triple threat is a man who can run, pass, or punt. A basketball triple threat is one who can pass, dribble, or shoot from the same position. The triple-threat shooter carries the ball chest high, with his knees slightly bent for driving, dribbling, or straightening up and shooting. (See Illustrations 1, 2, and 3 on page 55.)

If the player elects to shoot from this position (set shoot) he should hold the ball eye high for it to be lined with the basket. The arch should be put into the shot with a bending and straightening of the knees. Too many players line the ball with the basket and then drop the ball in the act of shooting. (Football coaches term this "pumping in passers.") This cancels the effectiveness of lining the ball with the basket. It is as illogical to do this as it is to aim a gun with the eyes and then shoot from the hips. (See Illustrations 4 and 5 on page 55.)

The knee-bending motion in the act of shooting has the effect of keeping the defensive man in doubt as to whether the shot will be taken or a drive-in will be made at the last instant. This doubt in the defensive man is highly desirable. It gives the shooter more distance from the defensive man and eliminates the necessity of wasting a man as a set blocker (or screener) in order to give the set shooter sufficient time to get the ball away accurately. (See Illustration 1 again.)

Two-handed set shot. Now to the mechanics of the oldest shot in basketball, the two-handed set—with both hands on the sides of the ball or with one hand under the ball and the other hand behind it. The latter method is often more desirable with boys who are unevenly muscled. Its use tends to eliminate lateral inaccuracy due to uneven lateral muscular pressure on the side of the ball. Some call this shot the stab shot, but actually it is a type of set shot. If either of these shots are taken, and they are generally taken from a distance of about twenty feet, the shooter should immediately slip into the foul line area for rebounding. Then he is taking the best combined defensive-offensive position in the front court. (See Illustration 1 again.)

Jump shot. If, according to the maneuvers of the defensive man, the player elects to drive and then shoot, he pulls the ball down in one motion from eye high and at the same time he puts it on the floor in a single dribble as far forward as possible in his drive-in. Then, at the conclusion of his dribble, he either jump shoots or lays up the ball, according to the distance he has gone and the congestion he has encountered. If he's still in congestion he will jump shoot with the ball a little higher than eye high, but nevertheless lined with the basket. (See Illustrations 1, 2, and 3 again.)

31

The use of this jump shot has revolutionized basket-ball shooting and defensive measures. But there is a tendency on the part of some players to overuse the jump shot. Many coaches believe the jump should be used mostly in congested areas in order to get over the defense, and in positions where it is not necessary to move in closer for rebounding maneuvers. Some shoot-ers have become so efficient in using the jump shot they employ it all over the court. Frank Selvy of the Na-tional Basketball Association is an example of this. His accuracy with the jump shot from almost anyplace on the court is amazing.

Pivot jump shot. The other shots employed in this pattern are the pivot jump shot and the pivot hook shot. The pivot jump has replaced the pivot hook in recent years because it allows for greater accuracy. The shooter gets a longer look at the basket and finds him-self in a better rebounding position, since he faces the basket at the conclusion of the shot. Paul Arizin uses the jump shot to great advantage, while Neil Johnston, also of the Philadelphia Warriors' professional basketball team, is a specialist in the turn hook shot. Both of these men have become highly proficient through untold hours of practice. It might be well to mention here that too much time cannot be devoted to shooting prac-tice. Both Arizin and Johnston have been known to return to the floor, after missing certain game shots, to continue practicing the shots they missed for as much as an hour. (See Illustration 6 on page 56.)

PASSING

Basketball has become more and more a game of passing. Formerly the dribble had been used to excess. Quite often the sole method of advancing the ball from the back court was the dribble. Now, however, the passing attack predominates for the simple reason that it is faster. And the dribble is now used largely to get the player into a better passing or shooting position. Or at special points in the game it is used as a time-consumer in "killing the ball."

It is not our purpose to rename and explain the fundamental passes of the game. But we do want to describe the various fundamental passes used in our pattern of incentive basketball. These passes apply to penetration of both types of defense, man for man and zone.

In our weave, cross-screening attack the ball is passed, half-passed, or handed off to a teammate just before the passer moves toward his teammate's opponent to effect a screen. The man who receives the ball thus is able to go in *two* directions. This pass is very important in the screen attack, as you will see when we get into pattern play. In making this pass *the passer should never look at his teammate, but rather at his teammate's defensive opponent*, whom the passer will attempt to screen after getting rid of the ball. (See Illustration 7 on page 56.)

At the same time the passer-screener must be able

to change his mind at the last moment. He either bounce passes to a prospective pivot man working inside from the corner, or he must be able to change his pass to a dribble-drive for the basket in the event the opening presents itself. The passer in the weave pattern may decide to give and go—that is give the ball to his teammate and drive directly for the basket instead of screening. Or he may give and screen in the opposite direction from the man receiving the ball. In both cases he changes his two-handed handoff—or one-handed bounce to the pivot man—to a quick push pass off his chest. This provides a faster surprise change of pace to take advantage of a weakness in the defensive setup.

In encountering zone defenses, the offensive men will often use push and one-handed bounce passes for a quicker change in attacking direction. In some situations, involving height advantages, the push volley pass is used. This is in the nature of a half-shot to your teammate. Quite often also, backboard passes can be made by banking the ball off the backboard to a teammate who is between the defender and the basket. This is used when it is impossible to get the ball to a teammate in any other way than by bouncing it off the boards.

Mention should be made that, in passing, the passer should be careful to observe the position of his receiver's defensive man so the defensive man will not intercept the pass. The receiver too should watch the position of his opponent and, if he is being overplayed, he should go for the basket. It is obvious then that two parties are to blame for interceptions in a situation of this kind: the passer who didn't observe the position of the defensive man and the receiver who didn't go for the basket when he was being overplayed. The old cliché of always moving to the ball does not always apply.

SCREENING

Screening is to basketball what blocking is to football. It involves freeing your teammate from his opponent. The difference is that, in football, contact is permitted, while in basketball no contact is allowed. The opponents must be given what we call escape room —about three feet. Keeping this in mind, the successful screener must move in such a way toward his teammate's opponent as *not* to touch him. He must try to cause this defensive man (1) to watch the screener and therefore lose sight of the man he is guarding, (2) to drop back to avoid congestion, or (3) to run into his own teammate. In one of these three ways the screener, by his movement toward the defender, releases his teammate for a set shot, a drive for the basket, or further pattern screening movements.

In effecting a screen, the screener should *continue* his movement—not set up a screen (pros seem to disagree)—at half speed so as to prevent switching or two-teaming of the offensive man. Another purpose of the screener's continued movement is to further utilize him in a second screen. Also, the more erect the moving screener can move, the more successful he is in obstructing the vision of the man he is screening. This places the defensive man at a guarding disadvantage.

The screener also should move directly at the teammate's opponent, watching the movements of the opponent. Then at the last split second he should give way in one direction or another so as to avoid the fatal contact that makes a legal screen an illegal block. Contact of this sort results in a charging or blocking foul call against you and loss of the ball. (See Illustration 7 again.)

The secret of successful screening is in watching the movements of the man being screened and *just evading* him. In a perfectly executed screen, the defending opponents often crash into each other, enabling the passer to follow any offensive course he desires. This successful screening can be accomplished only with hours of drilling, but it pays off in providing easier scoring opportunities.

Maneuvering Without the Ball

The ability of the player to maneuver without the ball is the mark of a great basketball player. Jim Pollard, George Mikan, Bob Cousy, and Tom Gola owe much of *their greatness to this ability*.

However, teaching the skill of "going without the ball" is a real problem for the college coach. The reason is that most high school stars become stars with the ball. They achieve publicity through their shooting, passing, dribbling, or rebounding. But in college they are told there is another road to greatness, and it's hard for them to believe it. They must now, at the college level, relate their movements to those of their teammates, *whether they have the ball or not.*

Assuming that the boy does not maneuver without the ball so as to keep his opponent occupied guarding him, the opponent quite often helps out his teammates with their men. Basketball therefore becomes a game, not of one man with the ball trying to beat his opponent, but of five individuals, all at the same time trying to outmaneuver their opponents, with and without the ball.

Combine these individual movements and you have the collective action of a team-functioning pattern. Therefore, the man without the ball should be head faking his opponent to (*1*) set him up for screening situations, (*2*) acquire backboard rebounding advantage, (*3*) acquire temporary pivot position, and (*4*) acquire cutting and reversing positions.

Let's assume a ridiculous (but not too ridiculous) situation. Suppose Number 3 in the offense of the five-man weaving offense is in possession of the ball and is trying to defeat his opponent and score. He will do this with a fake to the right and go left, with a fake to the left and go right, with a double fake and return to the right, or with a step directly at the opponent and back for a set or drive if his opponent rushes him. The same series of fakes and movements in a smaller way should be occurring in the other four positions. (See Diagrams 1 through 6, pages 38, 39.) Now ordinarily

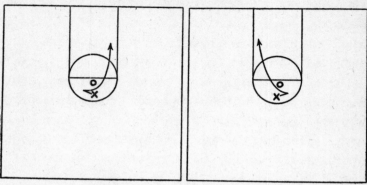

Diagram 1 (left). X with the ball fakes left, then drives right.

Diagram 2 (right). X with the ball fakes to the right, then drives left.

Diagram 3 (left). X with the ball fakes forward, then set shoots.

Diagram 4 (right). X with the ball fakes with the ball, gets set, then drives.

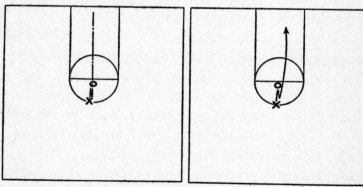

the other offensive men will not be able to dash to the basket. The defense will be playing them more loosely because they don't have the ball and don't pose an immediate scoring threat. However, assume that the four men without the ball walk directly toward the basket and remain there. If the defense is playing man-for-man tag, then the entire maneuvering area on the court is left to the man with the ball and his opponent. Games have been won with just this theory: *the one superior offensive man played the one inferior defensive man.* This hypothetical case should stress the importance of going and occupying the man without the ball.

A case in point occurred in the 1955 NCAA play-off game at Philadelphia between Villanova and Canisius. In the final seconds, with the score tied, Canisius gave

Diagram 5 (left). X with the ball fakes to the right, drifts to the left, stabs.

Diagram 6 (right). X with the ball fakes to the left, drifts to the right, stabs.

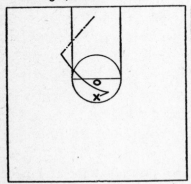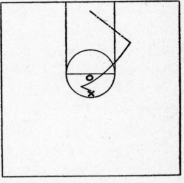

the ball to its best ball-handler and dribbler. The other four men took their opponents off in other directions. The one Canisius man had most of the court to operate in. Having all this room he drew a foul, made good at the line, and Canisius won. The four men without the ball helped as much as the man with the ball. They were doing things without the ball—keeping the defense out of the ball-handler's way.

Before a man in the rear court receives a pass from a teammate who is moving in to screen for him, he should head fake in the direction his opponent is over-playing him. This holds the defensive man in position before the offensive man receives the ball to go the other way on the outside weave.

The corner men on the five-man weave, who will become the rebounders after the ball has been shot from outside, should also fake along the endline just before the shot is taken, so that they can come back to the floor side for rebounding position. This same fake is used in seeking flash-pivot position, in moving in from the corners for jump shots, and in hand-offs to men cutting through the middle. In short, any pressure, in the form of starting fakes and moves that occupy the opponent, is highly desirable as part of overall team performance and maneuvering success. Without this collective pressure, the team is not a team but a series of individuals awaiting their turn to get the ball and put on solo unrelated acts.

The constant jockeying for position among all men

on a well-drilled team is beautiful to watch. And, although it is not readily discernable to the average fan, any defensive man who has played an opponent who knows what to do without the ball has had an unforgettable experience. High schools do little of it because they are over-occupied with teaching the fundamentals of passing, dribbling, and shooting. Colleges can do a little more of it. Some colleges do a lot of it and are highly successful. The pros do a lot of it if they are to become successful.

Dribbling

Dribbling, although it appears sensational and serves a purpose when used properly and not to excess, is not so dominant a part of basketball as most fans think it is. The reason for this is that too much dribbling promotes individualism. And individualism has a bad psychological effect on the rest of a team. Most players resent a dribbler who shows off. They feel he is hogging the ball. So they don't bother to try to maneuver without the ball. They feel the dribbler is so occupied with his dribbling that they will not be seen anyway if they free themselves to receive a pass. A dribble, therefore, should be used only in cases of emergency: to prevent traveling with the ball, to aid in taking a better screening or passing position, and to set for drive-ins in case opponents are out of defensive alignment.

In our screen-weave offensive pattern, particularly

in the front court, most of the maneuvering is done with the aid and use of a single dribble (one bounce) or, at the most, of two dribbles—one for a passing-screening maneuver and possibly one or two for the drive-in to the basket. Most young high school prospects are unbelievably surprised to learn that, with the proper shooting fake prior to their drive, they can go to the basket from a distance of twenty feet in one dribble. The secret of this, of course, is to put the ball down on the floor in front of your drive rather than to your complete right. Otherwise you give the faked defensive man a chance to recover his defensive position or to retreat to a better one. (See Illustration 3 again.)

The dribble provides an interval in which the offensive man can size up the defensive setup and still keep the attack moving. The series of weaves with one-bounce dribbles, short passes, and screens continues. This movement of dribble and pass does not have to be fast. It can be a half-speed movement. Then, if it is quickened when an opening presents itself, it furnishes a change of pace along with change in direction.

No attempt is being made here to discuss the use of the dribble in the mere advance of the ball to the point where the defense tightens. Nor will the value of a clever dribbler be discounted. He can "kill" the ball or draw a foul in the late minutes and seconds of the game that will save a victory or avoid a defeat. We have merely tried to relate the dribble properly to the overall pattern of the balanced weave-screen *incentive basketball* system.

It is significant that the Harlem Globetrotters insert Marquis Haynes or Leon Hillard into their lineup for show purposes. They are good entertainment. However, we are not interested in the dribble as a show performance. In fact that's what we're trying to avoid. Bob Cousy of the Boston Celtics in the NBA is one of those rare individuals who can properly handle excessive dribbling and relate his movements to those of his teammates. Cousy, one of the greatest of dribblers, does much of his maneuvering as showmanship in the professional league. Showmanship is required among the pros. But we in the college field are confined to the pure contest. We have no place for showmanship. Our purpose is to develop teams as teams, not individuals.

If the dribble is employed there are two positions from which it is started: first, from the triple-threat position and, secondly, from the low crouch that precedes a pressing defense. In the triple threat the ball is brought sharply to the floor with a down pull and with a forward or slightly sideward thrust. From this position the hand-off or pass-off into a screen is accomplished. (See Illustration 3 again.) The second method is utilized when the ball is being withheld from play in an effort to draw the defense out. The dribbler is in a low crouch with the ball held closely to the floor. He swings the ball back and forth across the knees before he starts his dribble on either side of the defensive man.

It is extremely difficult to stop such a dribble without fouling the dribbler, and it probably is the most effective way for an individual to kill the ball.

Any rear-court pivoting and dribbling should be discouraged for the obvious reason that any player reduces his overall team effectiveness by rear-court pivoting. During the interval his back is turned to his basket and to his teammates in the front court. He ceases to be an offensive threat until he has completed the dribble pivot and started in the direction of the basket, which after all, was and should be his constant objective.

During my summer of coaching in Puerto Rico, to stress the desirability of constantly facing forward I used the word *"Avanti!"* (the slogan of Garibaldi, the old warrior) meaning "ever forward." Quite often catch phrases or words like this are great teaching aides. Another one I used to discourage excessive dribbling was *"Exhibición!"* Needless to say, we managed to cut down on the excessive dribbling and rear-court pivoting after a while. And the team started to function as a team.

THE PIVOT PLAY

Rule-makers are making it increasingly difficult for pivot men to operate with the same degree of efficiency they had in the George Mikan, Bob Kurland, and Clyde Lovelette eras. These men were effective in pivot play because of their immense physical advantage over their opponents. However, many teams try to function with a pivot man but without a Mikan. They are, in effect, putting all their eggs in one inferior basket. If the pivot man is off in his shooting, they are beaten soundly. If he is making his shots, they win.

Believing that balance is the essence of the game of basketball, I have never used a set-pivot offense. Maybe if I had had a Mikan I would have. But let's look at the disadvantages of a set-pivot play. Anyone will probably agree that a moving target is harder to hit than a stationary one and that a set man is easier to defend against than a moving player. We will discuss the defense in a later chapter. Offensively, the set pivot man in hook-turn shooting does many things that are not desirable. Rule changes have moved him further away from the basket. He gets less opportunity to look at the basket than outside men. And, once having taken his shot, his momentum carries him away from the basket and hurts his rebounding abilities. Then too the introduction of the one-three-one zone defense largely has curtailed the use of the set pivot man.

But, more than technical objections to the use of the set pivot, I would like to voice psychological objections. As has been mentioned, the set pivot tends to become a one-man team with a four-man supporting cast. He makes a one-man game of what was intended to be a five-man game. This fact was more closely brought home to me while coaching the East team in the East-West All-Star games last year. Pivot specialists on both teams were thrown in with players who had played moving offenses. Two famous, highly publicized set-pivot players were completely inept and out of place against the moving offense employed by the East team. And I was told by several players, who were limited to outside maneuvers, how much more they would have enjoyed opportunities to move all over the court. They were limited in their movements because of the presence of the set pivot man, jamming the middle of the offensive court. The other men were relegated to the outside, less desirable scoring areas. They were the supporting cast to the star pivot man and they didn't like it.

When you go to a game sometime, just to satisfy your curiosity keep some statistics on the use of the pivot play. Record the number of times the ball is intercepted on the throw in to the pivot man, the number of shots missed by the pivot, the number of times Mr. Pivot is out of position for rebounding, the number of times outside men drop off their men and steal the ball or tie up the pivot into a held ball. Also record the number of times the pivot man has taken off-balance shots when someone else was in a better position to shoot. You'll be amazed at your statistics after several games. I know I was.

When I went to LaSalle to coach, they had Larry Foust playing the set pivot. We moved Foust out of the set-pivot play area, permitting a more balanced drive-through and more set shooting. We finished the season with a much better record than the previous season because of this balance. Even today Foust has greater value to the Fort Wayne Pistons because of his ability to move away from set-pivot situations.

When Tom Gola played in high school he was used in the set-pivot position, and rightly so, by his very able high school coach, Obie O'Brien. But, when Gola came to college where we had other tall men, we were able to allow him to develop evenly away from the set pivot. He became in my mind the greatest *balanced* basketball player of all time. Had he been relegated to the set-pivot position he might have become the greatest pivot player, instead of the balanced performer he is today.

Having dispensed with the discussion of the set pivot, let's go on to the discussion of the flash-pivot play, which is an integral part of our incentive-basketball, weave system to be discussed later. This flash-pivot play is executed by the men in the weave pattern playing near the baseline. They execute the usual fakes without the ball. They may head fake along the endline and then come back into the field of play in the pivot area for quick passes and jump shots. They may do any of the other fakes we have discussed in this chapter to obtain the flash pivot position, to rebound another's shot, or to drop back to the rear court and participate in the weave.

Once the player has reached the pivot area and has received the ball, his pivot shot can be in the nature of a turn hook shot or of a turn jump shot. Other shots are used according to the position of the defensive man. The important thing to remember in getting into an effective flash-pivot shooting position is that the two possible men executing the maneuver must time their fakes and movements so as to coincide with the outside screening men, who will feed the ball to them. The outside men must be in such a position that they will see the flash pivot enter the pivot area and can give him the ball quickly. (See Diagrams 7 through 9, pages 48, 49.)

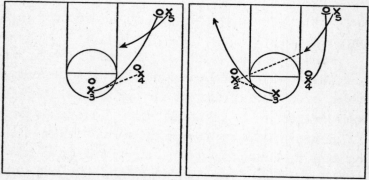

Diagram 7 (left). **3 screens 4's man and then 5's man. 5 goes to the pivot spot.**

Diagram 8 (right). **3 passes to 2 and screens. 2 passes to 5 on the flash pivot spot.**

Handing off the ball from the pivot has become less effective since switching, zone defenses, and other defensive measures have become more developed. However, the pivot shooter can increase his shooting

Diagram 9. 2 passes to 5 and then cuts off 5. 3 also cuts off 5.

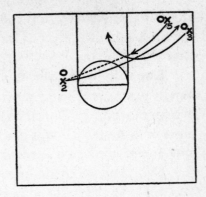

time by effective head and body fakes prior to releasing his shot.

FOUL SHOOTING

Foul shooting has become an increasingly important factor in the modern game of basketball. The bonus rule, which provided for an extra try on a one-shot foul if the first one was made, placed an even greater premium on good foul shooting. There are many instances where the losing team outshoots the winner from the field but loses the game on the foul line. So let's apply the rule of reason to this skill.

There is a law of physics that the most efficient machine is the machine with the fewest number of moving parts. Apply this physical law to the mechanical method of shooting fouls. It seeks to eliminate any unnecessary bending of the knees or arms, or any long muscular movements that allow room for more possible

49

error. The shortest and most comfortable movement should be used. (See Illustrations 8 through 11 on page 56.)

Logically then the elimination of knee-bending would make for greater proficiency, just as a minimum of arm movement would. With this reasonable law of physics in mind, we will grade foul-shooting minimum movements into two general classifications.

(1) The overhand eye-high stab method.

(2) The underhand lift shot, releasing the ball eye high.

The best illustration of the eye-high stab method is that used by Tom Gola. Gola has little if any knee movement and releases the ball on a line between the basket and his eye. This method is so logical and simple that it almost defies any elaborate description or discussion. Why players drop the ball and release it from any spot other than eye high makes no sense.

Shooting eye high shouldn't be too difficult, since this is the type of shot used in field goal attempts. You may bend a little at the knees to get more power in long set shots and in getting ready for a drive threat. So, in general, aiming habits do not have to be changed once the foul shooter steps to the foul line. But *the ball should not be released from any spot other than eye level.*

As for the underhand method, knee bending here also is cut to a minimum or eliminated entirely, if the shooter has enough leverage to throw the ball up without it.   To eliminate the variable knee bending distance —which adds to the possibility of error—the ball again is brought up and released at an eye-high level.   The underhand method is probably a more comfortable method and, since the foul-shooting interval should be a restful interval, a restful stance and method for the shooter is very desirable.   (See Illustrations 9 through 11 again.)

Many foul shooters prefer the underhand shot to the overhead stab because it is a nonmuscular tightening method.   However, it has the disadvantage of rarely if ever being used in general scoring from the floor during regular play.   The overhand shot is the common method of field goal shooting.   It might be significant, though, to point out that at one time the greater percentage of the first fifteen foul shooters in the NBA (including Al Cervi, George Mikan, and Joe Fulks) all shot their fouls with the underhand lift movement.

There are other ways to shoot fouls, but I don't recommend any of them.   Some shooters toss from behind and above the head.   Players jokingly call that the "radar shot," for it defies the theories of good fundamental shooting.   In many cases, players who make 75 per cent or more of their foul shots might do even better if they adopted the logical methods we have discussed.

Most coaches will not try to change a man who shoots fouls in an unorthodox fashion, as long as he hits 75 per cent or better.   One coach said his men could drop kick them in if they hit 75 per cent successfully. I am reminded of the story of Al Simmons of the Philadelphia Athletics, who hit with his foot in the bucket. Connie Mack never bothered to try and change the stance of a man like Simmons who hit .380 and better. I don't think we have to impress on anyone that a foul shooter hitting 75 per cent or better with his eyes closed shouldn't be ordered to open his eyes and drop to 50 per cent. But it might be worth a try to see if he could go to 90 per cent with them open.

So it would seem worthwhile to attempt to change the style of a shooter whose percentage of foul conversions falls below 75 per cent. I've seen foul shooters take angle positions on the line, moving themselves further away from their objective—the basket. Perhaps that makes them individuals, but creating individuals is not our aim. We seek to create teams, not individualistic performers. Many players learned early that balance is the important thing and that the simplest and most logical method of doing a thing is the best and quickest method.

I once had a player who shot about 70 per cent of his fouls successfully. He shot overhand. I felt he might do better underhand because he had such natural ability and coordination. He was dead set against any change and would go to the foul line, look over at me, and practically defy me. I felt he almost intentionally and carelessly would miss. Finally I said to him, "Okay, go ahead and shoot overhand. But if you miss *too* often we'll go back to the other method." Needless to say, his overhand foul shooting improved in his effort to prove that in his case I was wrong, and the end result was achieved by indirection. He improved his percentage shooting fouls overhand. That was all right by me.

As for practice methods for the individual, the thing to do is decide on the method most suited to the individual. Then have him stick to that method and practice it until the feel of the movement becomes a part of him. Most shooters start out as underhand foul shooters when they are youngsters because they can't get the ball to the basket any other way.

Most coaches will send a manager with a player who is weak on foul shooting and, during his off-class hours, will have the player shoot hundreds of fouls by the prescribed method. The manager returns the ball to the shooter, who remains on the foul line. It's important that the manager keep accurate records on the results of these practices and give these records to the coach.

Once the player gets the feel and the distance alignment, then he should move around the floor practicing other shots. At intervals he should return to the foul line and take a test shot. Perfection is obtained when, after shooting from various areas in regular field goal shooting practice, the player can go to the foul line and hit the first try. Then he has gotten in the "groove," so to speak. He has gotten the feel.

As for team foul practice, the best method is for

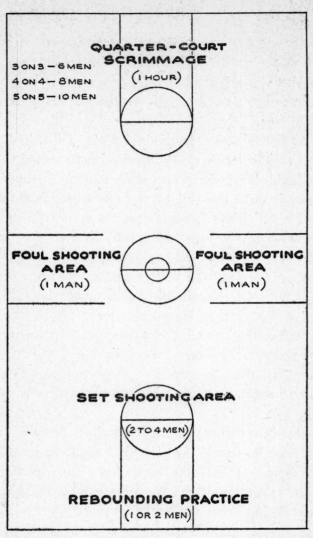

QUARTER-COURT SCRIMMAGE

(1 HOUR)

3 ON 3 — 6 MEN
4 ON 4 — 8 MEN
5 ON 5 — 10 MEN

FOUL SHOOTING AREA

(1 MAN)

FOUL SHOOTING AREA

(1 MAN)

SET SHOOTING AREA

(2 TO 4 MEN)

REBOUNDING PRACTICE

(1 OR 2 MEN)

Diagram 10. On a four-basket court three-against-three, four-against-four, or five-against-five quarter-court scrimmages can be held while the others use the other end basket for set shooting and the side baskets for foul shooting.

(Left to right) *Illus. 1, 2, and 3.* Tom Gola, LaSalle's three-time All-America, demonstrates the triple-threat ball-carrying position. He can shoot, pass, or dribble.

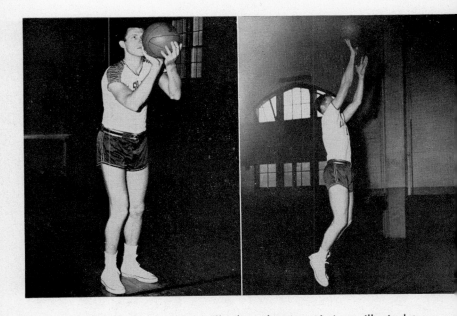

(Left) *Illus. 4.* Eye-high position of the ball when shooting. It is as illogical to align the ball with the basket and then drop it as it is to aim a gun from the eyes and shoot from the hips. (Right) *Illus. 5.* Gola jump shoots.

Illus. 6. The proper way to make a turn hook shot.

Illus. 7. Gola's eyes are on his teammate's defensive opponent.

Illus. 8. Letting the b on an overhead stab high foul shot.

Illus. 9. The underhand foul technique.

Illus. 10. Releasing the ball, by the underhand lift, foul shot method.

Illus. 11. Following hand lift, foul shot

Illus. 12. The side-slipping, moving-screen play, which forces defensive players (in dark jerseys) to fight through congestion to cover Gola with the ball.

57

Illus. 13. LaSalle's Fran O'Malley demonstrates drive-off-a-screen attack. Here he goes up in the air to hook a shot into the basket in the 1955 NCAA national semi-finals at Kansas City. Iowa Forward Carl Cain is unable to stop the shot.

Illus. 14. Alignment of five-man perimeter offense without a pivot. The ball is in the middle, with the screen to the right of the passer and the preparatory head fake by the offensive man opposite defensive No. 45.

Illus. 15. The moving screen in operation: screening by No. 23 who moves through to eventually screen for No. 99, who is head faking along the endline to set up his defensive man for the second screen by 23.

Illus. 16. In the event No. 45 anticipates the screen and overplays No. 44, the latter changes direction and cuts for the basket. No. 98 still continues to occupy his defensive man by head faking and maneuvering along the endline to prevent his defensive man from taking 44.

Illus. 17. In the event that No. 22 overplays his offensive man in the screen, his man may also give the ball to No. 44 and go to the basket to prevent overplaying the weaving attack.

Illus. 18. Here No. 22 continues on, after first screening for No. 44, and screens for the corner teammate, No. 99, who is about to receive the ball from the weakside man. (The weakside man has received the pass after the first screen from 44.) No. 99 may continue into the pivot position or on the outer section of the weave.

Illus. 19. If the middle man wants to start the weave to his right, rather than to his left, he may do so. No. 44 should be careful not to anticipate another screen and drift over to his teammate too soon, which would congest the center driving area for his teammate, the man with the ball.

Illus. 20. If the middle man starting the weave is overplayed by his defensive No. 22, he may drive to the endline after passing to No. 44. Then he may buttonhook for a pivot play and successive cutoffs by Nos. 99 and 44.

61

Illus. 21. In starting the weave, No. 22 may pass to the weakside, away from his screen, and with his strongside teammate apply a double screen for No. 99, who cuts off the corner for a pass and shot.

Illus. 22. The same double screen as in Illus. 21 on the left side of the floor.

Illus. 23. If No. 23 starts the left screen for his teammate to his left, his teammate, after cutting off him, may stop, double screen, and hand off to 23 again to cure a single switch.

the coach in his quarter-court screenings to call fouls and to intersperse his critical technique talks with foul shooting. The players try free throws while they are listening to criticism of floor play. Managers should record the misses, and players needing additional practice should stay late or come before the next practice session for individual practice in order to improve. (See Diagram 10, page 54.)

At practice sessions the day before a game five players stand at the basket, one at the foul line, and two on either side of the lane—similar to the way a team lines

Diagram 11 (left). Shuttle flash pivot (four-one offense): 2, 3, 4, and 5 have a series of outside screens of continuity interspersed with gives and goes and weakside screens. At an opportune opening 1 flashes into the pivot area for jump shots and hand-offs.

Diagram 12 (right) Three-two offense: 3, 4, and 5 cross screen. 1 and 2 flash into the pivot for rebounds, jump shots, and hand-offs.

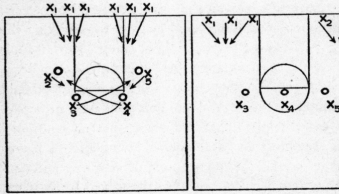

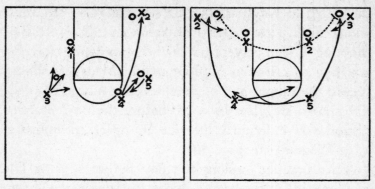

Diagram 13 (left). Unbalanced pivot offense: 1 and 2 alternate between playing the set pivot area and the baseline (with only one in the pivot area at any one time). 3 and 4 (with the ball) and 5 vary from cross screens and drives to pivot cut-offs.

Diagram 14 (right). 1 slides laterally through the pivot area and also sets the screens for the corner men, 1 and 2.

up for a foul shot. Then they rotate clockwise, each taking one foul shot. They keep a count of how long they can keep rotating without a missed foul. It's sort of a game and keeps up the boys' competitive interest. If someone misses, a big howl goes up for breaking the string. When the team can shoot about 25 or 30 fouls without a miss, they are as ready as they'll ever be.

There are times when you will find that a good field goal shooter is poor at the foul line. There is no reason for this other than that the player has an emotional block that must be overcome. Having such a player opens up one of the many facets of coaching and presents another problem that must be solved by coaches,

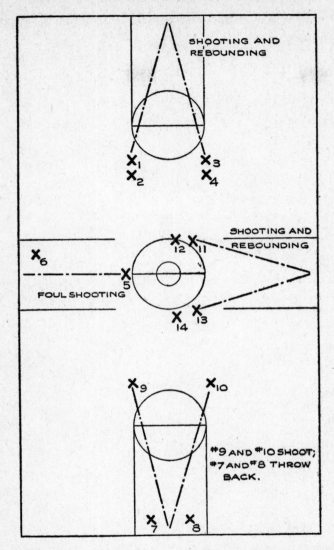

Diagram 15. Set shooting, rebounding, and foul shooting drill.

who, like other teachers, must be students of applied psychology.

★ 4

INDIVIDUAL DEFENSIVE SKILLS

F ROM THE PURELY TECHNICAL STANDPOINT DE-
fensive play should be easier to teach than offense, since
it is a system of merely checking the other fellow's
positive moves. But the recent youthful approach and
the thirst for the limelight has made it the most difficult part of basketball to teach. The headlines are
about the scorers. It's no different in any other sport.
In football you have the backfield stars and in baseball
the hitters. It is not surprising then that, when a good
defensive man is developed in basketball, he is something different.

Most basketball coaches will tell you that games
are won by defense. They try to have on their squads

at least one player who can hold the opposing scorers to a minimum of points. Such men were Al McGuire of the New York Knicks, Fred Scolari of the old Washington Caps, Bob Doll of the old St. Louis Bombers, and George Senesky of the Philadelphia Warriors—all professional players. Jim Phelan, one of my LaSalle players, was a master at defense, although he was only six feet, two inches tall.

Completely misleading is the player who scores 30 points per game, only to have his opponent score an equal number of points. Only the coaches, players, and discerning fans know this and appreciate the real value of defensive play. Some day in Utopia the headlines will be given to the great defensive stars, but that will only be in the "Utopia Gazette." *C'est La Vie!*

GUARDING

Now let's discuss the technicalities of defense, with guarding the first subject. Since the fundamentals of the standard guarding stance are so well known, I'll not go into them. However, since the proper guarding stance is generally agreed upon, I would like to add a few rules that must be followed in order to achieve guarding effectiveness.

The first rule of defense is to limit the movements of your opponent. Don't allow him to position you so that he can have the choice of going two ways. Overplay him to one side or the other, forcing him to go in the direction *you* want him to. This generally can be accomplished by playing your left foot opposite your opponent's left foot, if you want him to go right, or by playing your right foot opposite his right foot, if you want to force him left. The reason for this is that the opportunities for closer defensive playing are enhanced when the two-way fakes and feints of the offensive man are eliminated. In this way the guard can force the offensive man to go in the direction in which the guard can get the most help from his teammates, possibly via the switching maneuver. Overplaying also is employed against individuals who are habitual operators to the right or to the left. The idea is to force such players to move in directions in which they are less skilled. It makes them less efficient when they are forced to do so. (See Diagrams 16 through 20, pages 70, 71.)

The second rule for the defensive guard to remember is to position himself—with reference to his opponent—so as to keep the ball and his man in his line of vision as much as possible and always to be between his man and the basket. If this position is not possible to attain, then the next best thing is to set yourself in a face-guarding position until you can maneuver back to the preferred spot just referred to. This fundamental positioning will not apply in situations close to the defensive basket, where the offensive man is quite often individually zoned by playing between him and the ball.

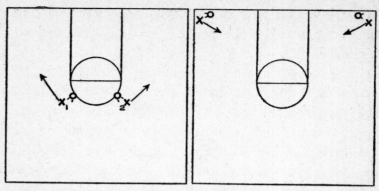

Diagram 16 (left). Defensive man 1 is playing with his right foot opposite his opponent's right foot to force him left. Defensive man 2 is playing with his left foot opposite his opponent's foot to force him right.

Diagram 17 (right). Defensive men 1 and 2 never let offensive men go along the baseline, but force them back into the field of play where defensive teammates can help.

Diagram 18 (left). Related man-for-man defense with defensive men overplaying. 1 is in possession of the ball.

Diagram 19 (right). 4 overplays his man to force him toward 1, 3, and 5.

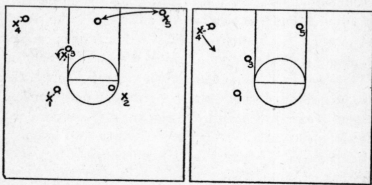

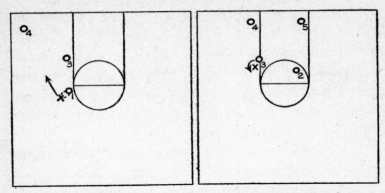

Diagram 20 (left). 1 overplays his man to the inside to force him to the sideline, away from the vulnerable middle, and also toward teammates 3 and 4.

Diagram 21 (right). 3 plays in front of his man to prevent a pivot throw-in and to invite a throw over him into the areas zoned by 4, 5, and 2.

Diagram 22 (left). 5 drops off to basket zone when the ball is on the opposite side of the court (as when it is in the possession of 1).

Diagram 23 (right). 2 drops off to the zone area of the foul lane to prevent a direct throw-in to 5.

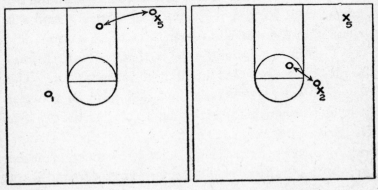

3.

A third rule of reason is that, the moment the offensive man starts a dribble, the first step of the cautious guard should be backward in continued retreat until the dribbler has ended his dribble. Then the guard should attempt to block the shot by either a jump or any other method consistent with the type of shot tried.

In the event a jump shot is attempted, then try your blocking via the defensive jump. Be careful not to jump directly at the shooter. Jump to either side of the shooter. In that way you'll prevent a charging or blocking foul. Jump with an arm extended across the area in front of the shooter's line of vision.

The "fight" through tag man-for-man defense is generally considered most efficient when the defense and offense are equal in personnel. This is particularly so because switching moves enable guards to alibi and avoid individual responsibility for a mistake. As a result I think most coaches use the tag man-for-man defense. However, against a good screening team the tag man for man has to adopt switching tactics. And this situation introduces additional rules of execution.

The first switching rule is that the man behind the play be responsible for calling the switch play. The play is moving away from him and he is in a better position to evaluate the play than his teammate is. (See Diagrams 24 through 27, pages 73, 74.) In all switching and guarding situations a lot of stress must be placed on impressing the boys that they must talk to and warn

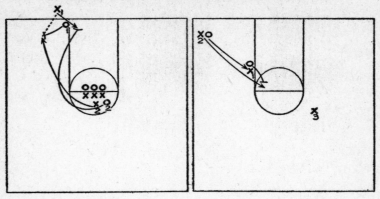

Diagram 24 (left). When opponents line up in this out-of-bounds play 2 intentionally chases his man around to 1, who switches to 2 as 2 receives the ball. Defensive 2 simultaneously switches to 1, who has stepped in from out of bounds.

Diagram 25 (right). If 2 cuts off the pivot he will make the switch call, because he is behind the play and better able to see the screen developing.

each other of impending block and screen situations. In this way the proper adjustments can be made. Each guard, in addition to watching his own man, must relate his defensive moves to the overall team defensive plan.

Still another important defensive chore is that of checking an offensive man on defensive rebounds. This is one skill that calls for endless practice to perfect your timing. It is highly desirable and pays off handsomely in ball recoveries during a game.

As the ball is shot, each defensive guard should step toward the offensive man, forcing him—if he follows the shot—away from the foul line area which is

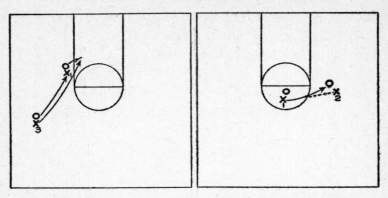

Diagram 26 (left). If 3 cuts off the pivot 1 will make the switch call, since he is behind the play and can see the screen developing.

Diagram 27 (right). If 1 starts the screening movement he will also make the switch call, because he is behind the play and is in the best position to watch the screen developing.

the most productive area for the recovery of defensive rebounds. If each defensive man does this and then continues into the rebound area, retaining his position between his man and the basket, he can make a pocket for rebound recovery. This is similar to the pocket a T-formation quarterback falls back into when he passes. In this way quite often taller opponents can be screened from rebounding the ball. Since it is illegal to accomplish this by contact, a legal checking-out procedure is a highly rewarding, but difficult skill. It calls for endless hours of practice, watching the ball in its flight and moving in toward the backboard, while at the same time keeping to the inside of your offensive opponent. It's not easy, but it's important and rewarding. Height alone in this procedure is not important. The ball must be watched in its flight toward the basket, the teammate moving in must be positioned, and the timely crouching position for jumping must be employed all in the right sequence before a guard can qualify as a real rebounding expert. (See Illustration 35 on page 100.)

☆ 5

TEAM OFFENSIVE
PATTERNS

You PROBABLY HAVE GATHERED BY NOW THAT I
am not a proponent of the set-play style of offense. A
set-play offense alone is easily defensed. Too, the set-
play offense leads you to the use of specialists like the
pivot. It takes away, at least from my point of view,
the genuine balanced team play. I believe that set plays
revolving around any one or two men tend to take the
interest of the game away from the other men on the
team. Of course, this hits on the very theme of this
advanced discussion of basketball techniques, *incentive
basketball.*

Any type of basketball pattern that involves the
use of set plays only and is dependent entirely on the
resetting of these plays is lacking in offensive balance.
When the set plays fail and have to be re-executed, the
defense has the opportunity to recover and reset to de-

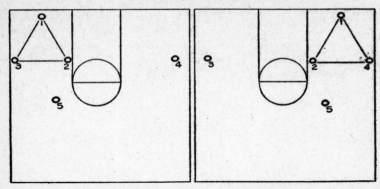

Diagram 28 (left). Standard zone attack with left overload.

Diagram 29 (right). Standard zone attack with right overload.

fend. The idea is to confuse and unsettle the defense and keep them that way. You can accomplish this only by using a *continuity offense, one that never allows the defense time to think, let alone rest.* (See Illustra-

Diagram 30 (left). The standard rebounding positions on a left shot.

Diagram 31 (right). The standard rebounding positions on a right shot.

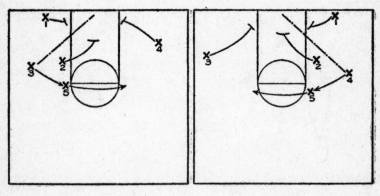

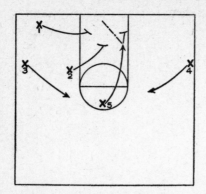

Diagram 32. Rebounding drive-through with proper checkbacks by 3 and 4.

tions 14 through 28, pages 58–62, 95–97.)

A set-play pattern defeats the very idea of the offense, which is to catch the defense out of position— off balance. You lose this opportunity with the set-pattern system. On the other hand, if you use a con-

Diagram 33 (left). 2 has been thrown an outlet pass because he was farthest down the floor and the nearest to the left sideline. Finding himself in that position when his teammate recovers the ball off the board, he must free himself by a dash.

Diagram 34 (right). Another alternative would be to make a quick, short dash and a buttonhook.

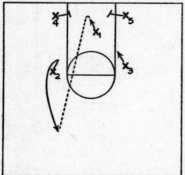

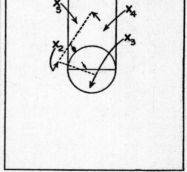

tinuity series like the screen weave, the defense has no chance to stop and regroup. Before they recover from the first maneuver, a second one is in process. The continuity offense keeps both the offense and the defense alive. It makes for a much more interesting game for the spectators and develops the thought processes of the players.

Lest I mislead you, let me say that set patterns are a necessary part of basketball as is the fast break.

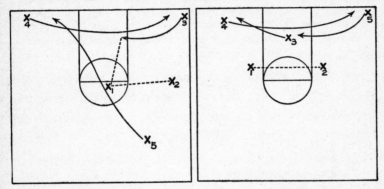

Diagram 35 (left). 2, unable to find 3, 4, or 5 free, repasses the ball to his rebounding teammate, 1, and they bring it up court.

Diagram 36 (right). Meanwhile 3, 4, and 5 are effecting inside screens in the front court.

(See Diagrams 33 through 41, pages 78–81.) But they should be used as a supplement to your moving offensive patterns. Set patterns are better for young, inexperienced players who are just mastering the fundamentals of passing, dribbling, shooting, cutting, reversing, and screening. Set plays are often introduced to

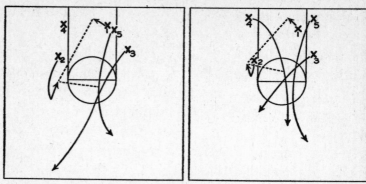

Diagram 37 (left) and 38 (right). 2 feeds the ball to the first quick breaker at approximately mid-court. Then 5 or 4 successively cuts through that area proceeds down court, and fans out after he has cut through the middle.

make them team conscious as an initial step toward a continuity offense. Set plays are used to defeat defensive blocks which have been thrown up to defeat the continuity offense. Remember, set patterns supple-

Diagram 39 (left). 3, 4, and 5 fan out to the corners of the offensive court and 4 starts the initial block (or screen) off 5.

Diagram 40 (right). Combating a press defense with an initial outlet pass, while 3 buttonhooks for a pivot pass.

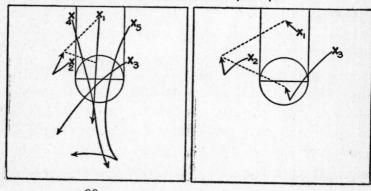

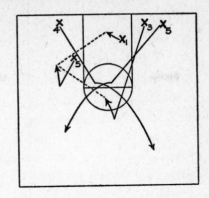

Diagram 41. Combating a press defense with 4 and 5 cutting off the pivot, 3.

ment the moving-pattern offense in order to keep the defense in a constant state of flux. They help to confuse the defense, which is the primary object of any offensive pattern.

The first fundamental plays in set-play patterns are the pivot plays with the long or high post. We have the situation where the pivot man is given unlimited time to operate in the outer half of the free throw area. Then we have the inside post, where a man may operate for a limited time only. And there are situations where other operations than the pivot are involved.

The main disadvantage of the high-post or long-pivot plays is the distance from the basket that the pivot man is required to operate from. This cuts down on the pivot man's shooting efficiency. Switching tactics are also made easier for the defense. In addition, the pivot man in this high-post position is easily checked off the backboard, cutting down on his rebounding effectiveness. The high post is desirable in killing-the-ball maneuvers. The high-post is also effective against pressing defenses, enabling you to utilize the standard double and single cutoffs off the pivot. Inside pivot plays are less effective now because of the rule that widened the foul lane. However, from a shooting standpoint, the inside pivot is more desirable since the post man is closer to the basket. He requires much closer guarding. This increases the need for much faster switch plays on the part of the defense.

Whether you use the long or the short post (outside or inside), any shooting done by the pivot man should be in the nature of a turn and jump shot rather than of a turn hook shot. The reason for this is that the hook shot draws the shooter away from the basket and cuts down on his effectiveness as a rebounder. This also permits outside defenders to play their men loose and double-team the inside hook shot pivot.

Set-play patterns involve the use of rear court set shooting and corner set shooting. Any number of set-play patterns can be evolved from almost any position on the court. However, the fact remains that any set-play pattern slows down the offense to the extent of allowing only one screen per play. On the other hand, in the moving continuity offense a series of screens are possible. Also a series of play situations are created.

SCREEN-WEAVE PATTERN

The screen-weave flash-pivot pattern offense is a compromise between the set play and random patterns.

Remember, your set-play pattern is weak because it allows the defense to readjust and recover after one play has been operated. The random offense fails to coordinate the thinking and maneuvering of the five men on the court. I believe the screen-weave pattern is a compromise between the latter two methods of offense.

Balance is the most important requisite in any attack. A team must have its players situated on the court so as to spread the defense and must allow itself ample space to maneuver the offense. Any team that permits itself to have four men on one side of the court is unbalanced. It defeats itself by congesting the area in which it wants to operate. In effect, by jamming one section of the court the offense limits its own ability to move in several directions.

Whether you use a five-man weave pattern, a four-man weave, or a three-man weave, the ball must be localized as close to the center of the court as possible. It is logical to assume that a greater defensive burden is placed on your opponent if you force him to defend from both sides of the court, rather than from only one. My teams start the weave from a semi-circle, with two men spread almost to the corners on each side of the center man, who has the ball. From this pattern we have our choice of a number of screens, give-and-go plays, set shots, pivot plays, etc.

The type of screen-weave pattern to be employed depends on four factors:

(*1*) The material available

(2) Defensive strength and personnel of the opponent
(3) The amount of time to play, which brings into consideration the physical condition of your players and the opponent.
(4) The personal foul count on your opponents and the score of the game (If you have several opponents with four fouls, it might be well to use a pattern that could force these players to foul out.)

Let's discuss each of these factors briefly. Assuming that all the players to be used in a screen-weave pattern have the same physical proportions, all the men on the team would execute each of the various skills an even number of times. Under these conditions each man might go through the pivot area approximately five times for jump shots and hand-offs. Each man, with good screening, might make five drive-ins to the basket. Each man might take five good set shots behind moving screens. And each man might recover the same number of rebounds off the boards.

On the other hand, if *one* of your men is unable to work the weave, to set shoot from outside, or to screen, but is adept at rebounding and corner shooting, the weave would have to be limited to four men. The odd man would then play along the endline (See Diagrams 11 through 14, pages 63, 64.) for rebounding, for corner stab shots, and for the occasional flash pivot with hand-offs or jump shots.

If you have *two* men unsuited to the weave pattern, they should be used inside to flash pivot, corner

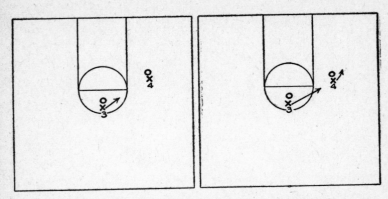

Diagram 42 (left). 3 has learned that he can't defeat his opponent, so he moves to screen for 4.

Diagram 43 (right). 4 head fakes his opponent right to set up a screen.

Diagram 44 (left). 3 continues on through, passing ahead to 4.

Diagram 45 (right). 4 drives left.

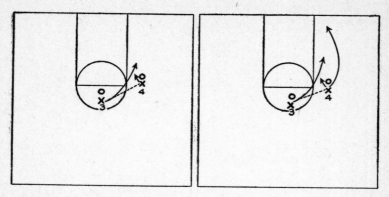

Diagram 46 (left). 4 head fakes left, setting up his opponent for the screen.

Diagram 47 (right). After head faking and receiving the ball, 4 drives right.

Diagram 48 (left). After 4 has head faked, 3 helps out by faking a screen on 4's opponent and driving.

Diagram 49 (right). After effecting the moving screen on 4's opponent, 3 goes to the corner to screen 5's opponent.

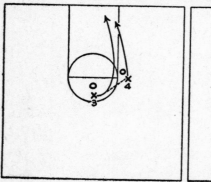
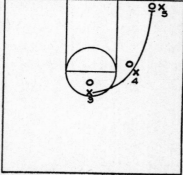

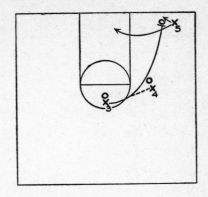

Diagram 50. After head faking his opponent, 5 drives for the bucket or flash pivot spot.

shoot, and rebound. But note that in the various types of weaves—five-man, four-man, and three-man—the middle is kept open to provide open areas for drives. This is the basis of *all* incentive basketball.

Should you find a defensive weakness in individual opponents, the weave would have to be adjusted to take advantage of that weakness. Shortcomings to look for are: the inability of key men to rebound effectively, their inability to defend against flash and other pivot plays, and their lack of sufficient defensive size. Any or all of these weaknesses may call for an adjustment of the weave into a three-man, two-man, or four-man pattern. The pattern, therefore, is determined by the weakness of the opponent.

Clock-watchers may be looked on with some distaste in the business world. But on the basketball court a player who doesn't know how much time is left to play hasn't got his mind on the business at hand. The period of the game or the time remaining to play may call for speeding up or slowing down the offense, depending on whether you are leading or trailing in the score. Assuming you are ahead, slowing up the offensive pattern consumes time and the passage of time operates to the advantage of the team in the lead. The defensive team ordinarily must force the play. Setting a high post (an outside pivot man), who can receive the ball from teammates being harrassed in the rear court, is an effective combined delayed offense and ball "killing" tactic often employed in the late minutes of a game.

Basketball is a grueling game and necessitates a change of pace in the attack to give some rest to key players. Ways other than regular time-outs and substitutions have to be devised to provide some of this rest. The simplest way to do this is to change the offensive pattern to a weave that permits one or two key men to rest along the end (base) lines, while continuing the four- or three-man weave. In that way the resting baseline men are still in position for rebounding. They still are in the game for defensive play, which calls for real hustling, since the offensive team sets the tempo. Hustle on defense and rest on offense!

Another situation that may call for a change in the weave pattern results when key defensive men have committed enough fouls to endanger their remaining in the game (i.e., five fouls). Some defensive men can't play well against certain offensive maneuvers. For example, a defensive player may not be effective against a pivot.   The idea then is to exploit this defensive weakness.   Vary the screen-weave pattern to force these weak defensive men to defend more often in their weak defensive skills.   The offensive team may cause the defensive key men to foul out of the game.   This playing to weaknesses with the use of adjustable screen-weave patterns becomes an important phase of team offensive tactics.

In summation, we first start with the five-man screen-weave flash-pivot offense and adjust into the four-one, three-two, or two-three, depending on the conditions just described.   It must be kept in mind *constantly* that in the employment of a screen-weave offense all men except the flash pivot, who is one of the corner men, completely face the basket in their maneuvers. They do this in order to be a constant offensive threat to each individual defensive player by keeping him so busy that he hasn't the time to help out a defensive teammate.

This is probably the most difficult thing to teach in the screen-weave pattern of play.   But once taught, each man remains a constant threat and an ever ready help to your key player, who cannot be double-teamed. If one of your men allows his defensive opponent to float in on a double-team maneuver, he defeats the system.   Part of Tom Gola's greatness was enhanced by the fact that his teammates, Charley Singley, Charley Greenberg, Alonzo Lewis, Fran O'Malley, Frank Blatcher, and Bob Maples, were all constant threats.

They all maintained practically the same shooting percentage as Gola because they constantly "fronted" the basket, even when screening laterally.

PIVOT PLAY PATTERNS

It is my feeling that a lengthy discussion of a pivot-play offense is like fighting the next war with the last war's weapons. For, with the increased number of big men in the modern game and with the rule changes that have widened the foul lane, the pivot play (the set-pivot play) is rapidly becoming outmoded as the dominating weapon in successful offensive basketball play. This will be discussed more fully when we get to team defensive patterns.

If, however, a set-pivot offense is to be used, it should be assumed that the pivot man is a better than 45-percent shooter on his turn hook shots. It should be assumed also that he is adept at turning and jump shooting and is quick on recovering for rebounding duties. It is probably safe to say that the pivot-play offensive pattern is just as good as the pivot man. He is the king pin of such an attack. If he doesn't know how to hand off, when and how to jump shoot and rebound, and when to hook shoot, the pivot offense is not as desirable as some others.

It is my feeling that the big man, six feet, eight inches and taller, is of greater value on defense than on offense. This is due to recent and pending rule changes. Probably by the time of this publication, or shortly thereafter, more restrictions will have been placed on the big pivot man on offense. A recent change is the widening of the foul lane to 12 feet. It is possible that the tap-in may be eliminated and rebounding curtailed by a rule requiring the ball to be passed out before a second shot is taken. Some wag has even suggested that the little man be allowed to stuff the ball through a hole in the floor under the basket and thereby be credited with two points. The big man would undoubtedly experience the same frustration trying to stoop to defend against the little man that the little man faces when he tries to defend against the "funneling" of the ball into the basket by tall men like the fabulous Bill Russell of San Francisco.

Other texts have provided any number of set play patterns, the most common of which are diagrammed. However, in introducing the double screen off the pivot-play pattern, devotees of this style have increased the effectiveness of the system. This effectiveness has recently been cut down by the use of proper switching and related defensive play, which will be discussed in Chapter 6, Team Defensive Patterns.

COMBINATION PATTERNS

Coaches not blessed with the type of material they need for their ideally balanced offenses are forced by

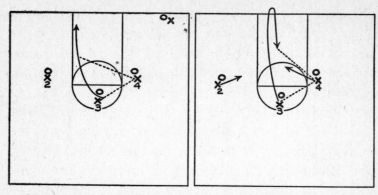

Diagram 51 (left). If defensive 3 overplays offensive 3, the latter gives to 4 and goes to the basket for a return pass.

Diagram 52 (right). If the defense recovers, 3 goes to the baseline to execute a buttonhook and flash pivot, with the usual cut-offs by 2 and 4.

Diagram 53 (left). 3 effects a weakside screen on 4's opponent.

Diagram 54 (right). A variation using the weakside double screen.

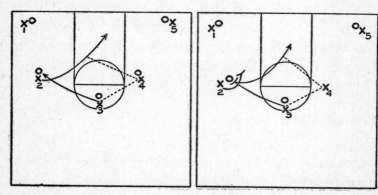

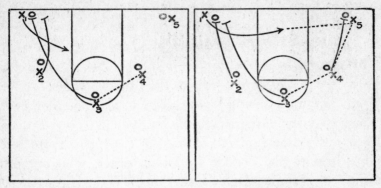

Diagram 55 (left). 2 and 3 execute a weakside double screen on 1's opponent.

Diagram 56 (right). A weakside double screen and a strongside single screen, with a pass to 5 before screening his opponent.

necessity to adopt a combination pattern. (See Diagrams 57 through 59, pages 94, 103.) This system involves several scorers, generally the little outside men, and bigger inside men. The little fellows are guards and the big men forwards and centers. This is true generally for the reason that in high school the big men have been developed along stationary pivot lines because of the eagerness of the high school coach to get the ball off the backboards. So the big boy is constantly near the boards for rebounding.

A fallacy can be detected in this system. The presence of the big man inside at all times, or near the basket at all times, necessarily attracts big defensive men. If neither the offensive nor the defensive man has assets other than size, it becomes a Mexican stand-off. The sizes cancel each other out. It would be much better to exploit the weakness of the opponent's defensive men by playing with an adjustable offense like the one described in the screen-weave flash-pivot offense.

If a combination pivot-screen attack is desired, two men play the corners constantly, flashing into the pivot for jump shots and rebounds. Occasionally there is a hand-off to the outside feeder-screeners, who cut off the flash pivot for drives or set shots. If the corner men, who play the same corners and rarely participate in the outside weave, are not successful in their flash into the pivot, they return to the corner for a new sally into the

Diagram 57 (left). If defensive 5 plays offensive 5 loose and jams the middle of the weave pattern, 3 passes to 5 and set screens for 2. 2 then cuts into the pivot position to receive a pass and cut off from 5. After screening 2's opponent, 3 goes on to screen 1's defensive man.

Diagram 58 (right). 3 passes to 2 while both 3 and 4 double screen 5's opponent. Then 2 passes to 5, coming out behind the double screen.

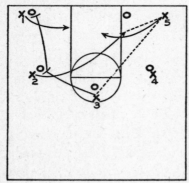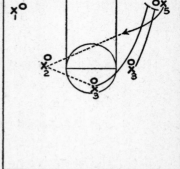

Illus. 24. When starting the weave, No. 24 may change his mind about screening for his teammate to his right and may fake the screen and bounce to No. 99, flash pivoting out of the corner. Note that No. 44 (opposite defensive man No. 45) fakes 45 away from the pass.

Illus. 25. No. 24 completing the weakside screen after passing the ball to his right to No. 44, who passes to 24's teammate for whom he has screened.

Illus. 26. If No. 99's defensive man drops off him in the corner, the middle man in the weave will pass to the corner man, No. 99, and screen for the teammate to his left, who is about to receive the pass from 99.

Illus. 27. Double cutoff by the outside weavers past the flash-pivot corner offensive man, No. 99. Note other offensive players checking back for defense.

Illus. 28. After an outside screen, the outside man cuts to the pivot area and receives a pass from the corner man, No. 99. No. 99 then cuts off of the pivot man, who has started originally from the rear court after the screen. No. 44, the original screener, has continued on to the corner screening 99 (in black), whose opponent takes a handoff from No. 99 in white.

97

Illus. 29. The modern game is a big man's jump-shooting contest quite different from the game of thirty years ago. Every man in this picture is six feet, four inches tall or better. This is action in the December, 1952 LaSalle–Stanford game.

Illus. 30. A perfect example of the underhand layup shot—made by LaSalle's Charley Singley in the final NCAA championship game at Kansas City against Bradley in 1954.

(Left) Illus. 31a. Poetry in motion: Gola in action against Millersville (Pa.) State Teachers College and (above), Illus. 31b, against Muhlenberg.

Illus. 32. Most coaches object only to officials' calling fouls that they are not in position to see. Not so with this official, Jocko Collins, who was right on top of the play. Collins is now head official of the NBA. Here Newt Jones of LaSalle is being fouled in the Cincinnati game of 1951.

Illus. 33. The middle of the zone is sometimes its weakest point—LaSalle–Stanford action, 1952.

Illus. 34. Jim Tucker (No. 4) and Dick Ricketts (No. 12) of Duquesne and Jackie Moore of LaSalle in action at Madison Square Garden in 1952.

Illus. 35. How to crouch and watch the ball while rebounding. This is the LaSalle–UCLA game at Madison Square Garden in 1954.

Illus. 36. Everyone is playing the ball but Seton Hall's Walter Dukes, who is playing Tom Gola—in the NIT game at Madison Square Garden in 1952.

The Evening Bulletin, Philadelphia

Illus. 37. Overpassing by Charley Greenberg in the LaSalle–Princeton game, March, 1955. Greenberg should have shot the ball when he was that high, instead of passing off to Gola. Note the position of his hands on the ball.

102

Illus. 38. Three members of a LaSalle basketball team: (left to right) Norman Grekin, Jackie Moore, and Frank O'Hara.

Illus. 39. The LaSalle bench after the 1952 St. John's game in the NIT at Madison Square Garden.

Diagram 59. 3 passes to 5
and set screens for 4. Then
4 cuts off and sets a second
screen for 3, who cuts through
to receive a feeding pass
from 5.

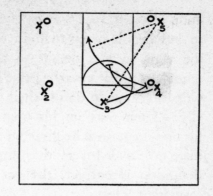

pivot area when an opening occurs or when their defensive men fail to cover them properly.

It should be fairly obvious that in this kind of offense the corner men who will become the flash-pivot men must become highly proficient at corner set shooting. They should approximate 45 per cent in order to prevent their defensive men from dropping away and helping out on the outside screeners, who have driven down the middle to score. It is my feeling that, if time, skill, and physical attributes do not permit the use of the five-man screen-weave flash-pivot system, some combination is the next most effective system. However, the two corner men must be able to shoot effectively.

RANDOM OFFENSE

Many coaches use the term "random offense" very loosely because they want to take the easy way out. They don't want to drill in systematic patterns. Random, I take it, means every man's doing what he wants to do when he wants to do it. I suppose each boy plays the way he was taught to as an individual in high school. In that case the game becomes one of five individuals trying to defeat their five opponents individually. Each puts on his own unrelated show against his opponent until he gives up the ball and lets his teammate take over for another single performance. If this definition is correct, the very essence of basketball, team play, is lost.

However, even in random offenses, where the individual predominates over the team concept, certain fundamental rules must exist so that the individuals can operate with maximum efficiency. These rules are:

(1) The ball and player must operate mostly from the middle of the court (midway between the sidelines) so as to permit varied directional operations.

(2) The back of the operator should never be turned toward the offensive basket in the rear court.

(3) There must be a minimum of two players close enough to the offensive backboard to handle offensive rebounding.

Random's being what the word generally means makes it fairly obvious that any further discussion of this type of offense would merely lead to a confession that the college coach who teaches this kind of play should turn his salary over to the high school coach who taught the boys their fundamentals and permitted them to play as individuals and at *random*.

TEAM OFFENSIVE PATTERNS

SET PLAYS

In addition to the moving and set-play patterns discussed so far, the college coach must and does evolve

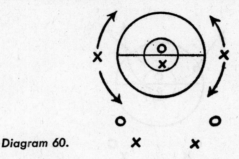

Diagram 60.

set plays from held-ball and out-of-bounds situations. These patterns quite often are highly effective and result in a key score or in the retention of the ball. You

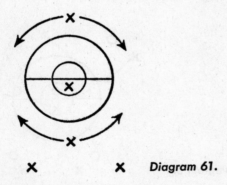

Diagram 61.

can't score without the ball, you know. There are any number of signal methods employed—hand signals, numbers, foot signals, etc. The signals can be given by key players on the team. All the signals are prod-

ucts of the coaches' imagination. I will set up and describe one system of held-ball signals and one series of
out-of-bounds plays that might be thought-provoking.
(See Diagrams 60 through 68, pages 105–108.)

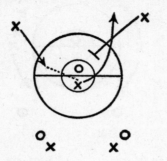

Diagram 62.

In the held-ball situations it should be obvious that
the jumper should tap the ball to a teammate who has the
height advantage over his opponent. The man receiv-

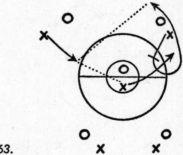

Diagram 63.

ing the tap should be in an area where he is or can get
free to take the ball after the toss-up is tipped his way.
Let's assume then that the jumpers are standing in the
center of an imaginary clock, with twelve o'clock in

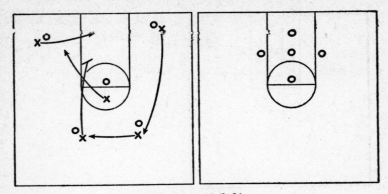

Diagram 64 (left).

Diagram 65 (right). Defensive area tips.

front of the jumper, six o'clock behind him, three o'clock to his right, and nine o'clock to his left. These numbers together with the other numbers on the clock are the positions that the ball will be tipped to.

The teammate to receive the tipped ball will be

Diagram 66 (left). Side out-of-bounds play.

Diagram 67 (right). Offensive area tips.

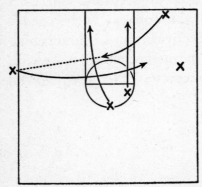
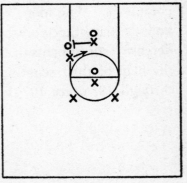

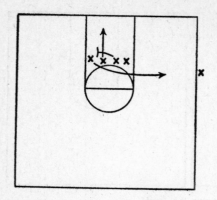

Diagram 68. Side out-of-bounds play.

designated by the jumper before he takes the jumping stance. The jumper looks at the intended receiver and calls a number on the clock (i.e., 1, 2, 3, 4, 9, 12). When the ball is tipped, the teammate moves to that position and receives the ball. However, in designating the floor position the tipper should be sure that the area of the floor is open. He shouldn't tip to a congested area.

The out-of-bounds play doesn't call for a discussion other than a few illustrative diagrams and some brief comments. The more variables present in the out-of-bounds play, the more effective it is in counteracting defensive adjustments that the opponents will make with the help of their scouting reports. (See Diagrams 66 through 78, pages 107–112.)

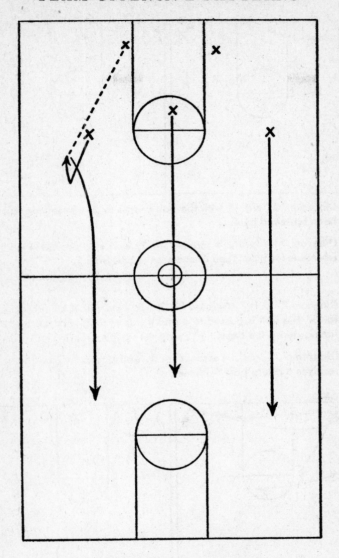

Diagram 69. **Three-lane quick break from zone.**

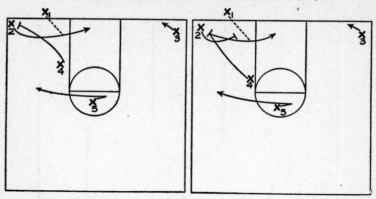

Diagram 70 (left). 1 with the ball passes to 2, whose man has been screened by 4.

Diagram 71 (right). 4 screens for 2, who cuts around 4 and rescreens for him. Then 4 receives the ball from 1.

Diagram 72 (left). 4 screens for 2, who cuts and in turn screens for 3. The ball is passed to 4 and 4 passes to 3, who has been faking along the baseline to help set up 2's screen.

Diagram 73 (right). 4 screens for 1, who passes to 2 and then receives a return pass from him.

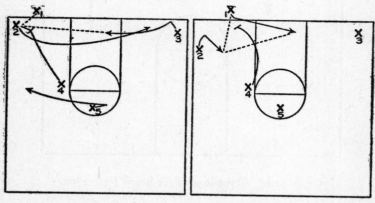

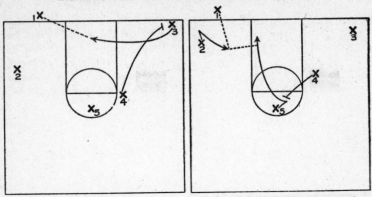

Diagram 74 (left). 1 passes to 3, whose man has been screened by 4.

Diagram 75 (right). 4 backward screens 5's man. 5 head fakes right and then cuts off to the left, receiving a pass from 2 (or directly from 1).

Diagram 76 (left). 4 screens for 2, who, together with 1, sets up a double screen for 3. 3 fakes right, cuts left around the double screen, and gets the ball from 4 (or 5).

Diagram 77 (right). Again 4 screens for 2, and 1 and 2 set up a double screen for 3. But this time 3 fakes left and then cuts right around the double screen to get the ball from 4 or 5.

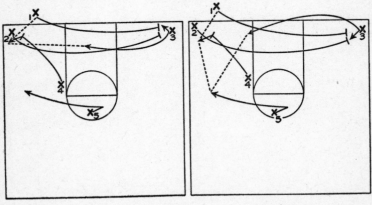

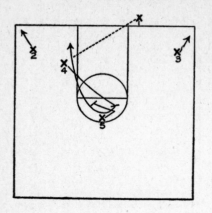

Diagram 78. 4 backward screens 5's man. Then he fakes right and goes left to set up a second screen for 5, who drives in off the second screen and gets the ball from 1.

6

TEAM DEFENSIVE PATTERNS

IN THE EARLY DAYS OF BASKETBALL EACH MAN WAS responsible solely for his immediate opponent and no one else. He tagged him all over the court and in turn was tagged all over the court by his opponent. Then, with the advent of the pivot and screen plays, the defensive man quite often found himself running into his own teammates in his efforts to tag his man. It gradually dawned on the defensive man that he had to watch other things than his immediate opponent. He gradually took up a defensive position that prevented his getting lost in the screen-and-block shuffle. He began to relate his defensive moves to those of the rest of the team to: (1) prevent himself from being caught in the congestion, (2) enable himself to help his teammates occasionally with their opponents, and (3) force his opponent to go in directions that were advantageous to the defense. Objectives (2) and (3) are included in "related defensive play" and develop into zone defensive play.

Many coaches prefer the man-for-man tag defense with some related moves, for the reason that in the tag system defensive responsibilities for certain key men can be definitely placed. Failure of the defense in man-for-man tag embarrasses the defensive man and causes him to put forth greater effort in his job.

Defense is composed largely of two elements: condition and determination. Both are unrewarding attributes insofar as personal glory is concerned. The defensive man seldom rates the headlines. As in many other sports, the awarders of cups and other honors generally have eyes only for the scorers. But defense sometimes is more important than offense. Many coaches will tell you that the game is won by the defense.

The tag defensive method encourages the offense to screen itself, and the game becomes a contest of reactions between the screeners and the defensive boys attemping to fight through to recover their men. Situations like this provide the very best entertainment and challenge in highly technical basketball.

Moving on from the tag defense into the trading of men, we encounter the word "switch"—the device used to counterbalance offensive screening. This switching, to be accomplished perfectly, calls for the defensive man behind the screen play to call the switch.

This call should be consistent with the overall idea that, on defense generally, teammates behind the play should talk consistently to warn their defensive mates against impending, disastrous screening situations being set up by the opponents. (See Diagrams 25 through 27, pages 73, 74.)

In forcing the offensive man to go in a direction beneficial to the defense, the offensive man is exploiting and playing to the offensive man's weakness. You should try to force him either toward defensive help or in a direction in which he moves with less efficiency. Most right-handed men move better to their right than to their left because they have done that more. It reminds you somewhat of football some years ago when the defensive left halfback was always the best tackler in the backfield and was placed there because the offense ran to its right more often.

However, there is more to be considered than mere overplaying to exploit individual offensive weaknesses. You should try to force the offense to limit its activities to certain areas of the court, to the exclusion of other, more desirable offensive areas. An illustration of this is the defensive outside guards' overplaying the offensive feeders to the inside to keep them out of the middle— the most desirable offensive area. It is easier to operate offensively from the middle of the court (midway between the sidelines) because you can go in two directions. It is also easier to feed a pivot man from the middle. (See Diagrams 16 through 23, pages 70, 71.)

The corner defensive men should overplay their opponents along the baseline to prevent them from driving along the endline. In the latter case the endline guard can see the ball and the pivot plays developing, and can help out on the pivot man. Also he can drive his man back toward the center of the court where he had more defensive switching help. This kind of defense was largely responsible for LaSalle's losing only one game in six years to a set-pivot team offense. That one was lost to Kansas in a close game during the Olympic trials final. The giant, Clyde Lovelette, starred in the pivot for Kansas in a game we led for 37 minutes, with our best pivot guard, Jackie Moore, not playing because of the death of his mother. We had to play a strange pivot defender against Lovelette who wasn't as practiced in fronting the pivot men.

THE ZONE DEFENSE

Now we turn with mixed emotions to the highly controversial zone defense. (See Diagrams 28 and 29, page 77; 79 through 84, pages 118, 119.) This defense is in the twilight zone for it is difficult to define when viewed in the same light as the switch or the trading of men by the defense. Critics of the zone have difficulty defining what a zone is as differentiated from switching men. For example, if two defensive men trade men and switch, it is defined as a switch and desirable. If three men do the same thing, it is still a switch. If four trade men according to the movements of the opposition, it could logically be termed a quadruple switch. But, if five men trade, is it a quintuple switch and desirable, or a zone and undesirable?

I would like to make my position clear on the zone, whichever way it is defined. I will do so by first confessing that anything that takes the speed and movement of the man out of the game decreases the interest, since basketball started out to be primarily a game of speed. However, any team should be permitted to use any fair method to accomplish its purpose. And it is the responsibility of the offensive team to counter with specialized methods to accomplish *its* objective: to win fairly. Any legislation robbing either the offense or the defense of particular maneuvers would tend to stereotype the game and deprive the teams and the players of *individuality*, which is the very essence of sport. It would be just as sensible to regiment us all to wearing orange ties or to living in identically styled houses.

But the zone, whatever way it may be defined, has a tendency to equalize physical and material differences. Although it takes the speed out of the game and turns it into a duel of passing, it has been the determining factor in a number of major basketball upsets. And the spectators like to see upsets, for most people favor the underdog. Real champions in every sense of the word should have sufficient balance and know-how to compete against all types of defenses. If they don't have that balance, they are not the real champions they should

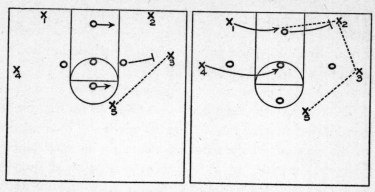

Diagram 79 (left). **Specialized attack against the one-three-one zone with right overload.**

Diagram 80 (right). **The defense retaliates by shifting to cover the area left open by the offense's attack.**

Diagram 81 (left). **Still combating the zone, the offense will pass to whichever man is left open by the defense's shifting.**

Diagram 82 (right). **Position of the offense before attempting penetration of the zone to the left.**

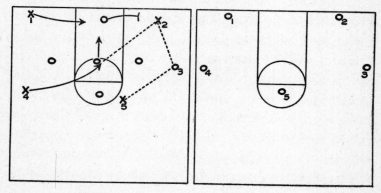

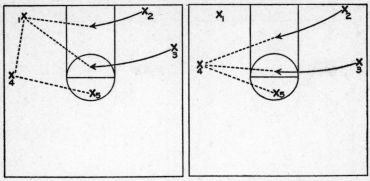

Diagrams 83 (left) and 84 (right). Movements of the defense against the attempted penetration of its zone to the left.

be. (See Diagrams 85 and 86, page 120.)

With these observations as an introduction to the discussion of zones, let's list the general types of zones in use, and mention also the particular advantages in the use of each.

The two-one-two. This zone defense was used last year more often than in other years and probably will be called upon even more frequently in the future because of the widening of the foul lane. The widening of the lane restricts the movements of the offense in this area. A two-one-two zone is employed generally by teams with only one big man. He serves as a sort of goaltender or as a rebound net, if he isn't tall enough to block the first shot. This zone concentrates the defensive strength in the middle areas of the court and permits the check-out on rebounds of single pivot men. It also permits a three-man front quick-break line in the

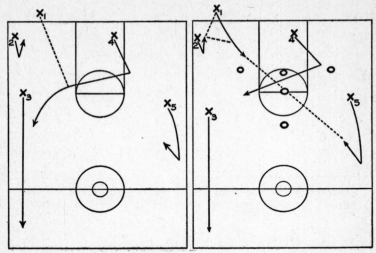

Diagrams 85 (left) *and* 86 (right). **Moves against a zone press set up by Penn State in the semi-final play-offs at Kansas City in March, 1954.** Two offensive men go deep in their own territory to freeze the back zone man in position. Then one of them buttonhooks at half-court, goes directly at defensive man 4, and cuts right to receive a pass from 1. There are then three offensive men on two defensive men. In Diagram 86, when defensive men 1 and 4 double team one of the offensive players, he passes to a teammate, receives a return pass in bounds, and then passes to a teammate who is buttonhooking. This again puts three offensive men against 3 and 5, restoring the offense's three-on-two advantage.

event the ball is shot from one of the corner spots.

The three-two. This zone centers around two big men and is designed for inside board strength and for a fast-breaking front line. Three-two zones are employed when the defensive teams have sufficient board strength in two big men. This leaves the corners open for set shooting and does not provide for good checking out of the key pivot offensive men. However, it does give added fast-break front-line strength in the event a shot by the offensive team is missed and is picked up from out-court. In effect, the defensive team is gambling that its two back defensive men will be able to handle the board rebounds and inside shooting, in order that its front three can break quickly going from defense to offense with three on two.

The one-three-one. The overemphasis of the big man in the pivot sent coaches scurrying for ideas to cut down the effectiveness of the post. The one-three-one was evolved and it practically put the set pivot man out of business by zoning him with one man in front and one behind him. True, the weaknesses of this defense are the corners and the outside areas. The outside areas comparatively close to the basket are vulnerable for the offense. But there is no question that the one-three-one cuts the effectiveness of the pivot man. In this defense, as in all zones, once the ball is moved into the baseline area by the offensive team, the defensive alignment becomes a two-three zone.

The two-three. This alignment is used to concentrate the defensive strength close to the basket. It doesn't provide much for quick-break opportunities. It is weak in that it is easier to get the ball in to the pivot man than it is in some other defenses. But this defense does provide corner strength, along with the opportunity to shuttle in and out the middle defensive man. Still, the outside court areas are weak and open for effective close set shots.

The one box. As we have said before, in a strict zone defense the defenders defend areas of the floor rather than individuals. However, drifting away from the standard zone, we have a situation where one defensive man will play a man-for-man tag defense against the star scorer of the offensive team. His teammates will play areas of the court in a box formation against the other four men of the defensive team. In this way, if the star offensive man escapes from the defender who is tagging him, he is immediately picked up by one of the men in the box. Princeton has used this kind of defense against some famous Villanova stars with great effectiveness.

Combinations. Any number of combinations of man-to-man and zone are used, depending on what the coach wants to accomplish. Some coaches, against teams with individual stars, prefer the three-two zone, with a defensive man in the area where the star is operating playing the star man to man while he is in that zone. When the star shifts his operations to another part of the zone, another defensive man picks him up and plays him man for man until the star leaves that zone. With this method the defensive fouls incurred while playing the star are distributed among several defensive men.

Much discussion has arisen as to the legislation against the zone defense. Many of us are wondering how the zone can be legislated against when it can't be defined.   As I've pointed out, the line between a switch and zone is so fine that it almost defies distinction.   The officials, being only human, have enough of a problem enforcing the already complex judgment rules of this great and complicated game.

Good teams with the proper balance will be equal to the zone.   Actually, it becomes a coaching problem rather than a problem for the rule-makers.   In LaSalle's final game against San Francisco in the 1955 NCAA tournament at Kansas City, we tried a zone.   But San Francisco had the men and means to cope with it. They deservedly won the game and the championship.

In recent years the zone has been used as more than a defensive weapon.   A quick switch to a zone, even though you may be behind in the score, can upset a team's offensive maneuvers and enable you to score quick field goals.   One year, when the University of Arizona led LaSalle in a National Invitation Tournament game, we switched to a three-two zone.   Using the three-two, we intercepted several of their passes and turned them into quick field goals that changed the complexion of the game.   In the Holiday Tournament in New York last year, we did the same thing, with the score against us by four points, and caught the UCLA team off balance.   They were not accustomed to playing against this type of defense and we were very fortunate to go on and win against a very fine California team.   So many coaches can also play the zone defense as a surprise offensive weapon.

Another use of the zone is to keep key players from fouling out of the game when they are burdened with an excessive number of personal fouls. The coach, by using the zone, can keep the player who is burdened with personals away from the rough action where he might commit the foul that would put him out of the game. This allows you to keep your key performers in for offensive maneuvers.

The final NCAA game in the 1954 championship tournament at Kansas City between LaSalle and Bradley illustrates this final point. Tom Gola had four fouls on him early. We moved him to the corner of a two-three zone and put a substitute in the middle to absorb the board work and the fouls that go with it. Gola remained to finish the game. These are the moves that all coaches make, and they are moves that make basketball the fascinating tactical game it is.

7

TRAINING

UNDER NCAA REGULATIONS TWENTY DAYS OF organized spring practice are permitted. In the fall no organized practice is allowed before November 1st. These rules were intended to de-emphasize the sport. But anyone connected with boys who love to play basketball knows they can't be kept away from the court. It is rather amusing that some educators think the modern boy, deprived each day of several hours of athletic exercise, will put those hours on his studies. It has been my experience that those free hours will be idled away in some less productive manner. The boy may even chafe at the thought that he is being deprived of the right to exercise—a right inherent to any red-blooded boy in the teen years of his life.

PRE-SEASON TRAINING

Some educators go to the other extreme. They

hold that the boy is a better student if he works off some of his excess energy. But it is my belief that real athletes never let themselves get far out of condition. They'll do something to hold their physical edge. Normal physical training shouldn't stop and start with the formal season. It would be well for all of us to keep physically fit so that we will function better mentally. Getting back to the basketball picture, it is often desirable for basketball players to play soccer or run in intramural cross-country during the off-seasons to build up their legs and stamina. Some coaches favor jumping rope. Others believe in calisthenics to build muscle coverings over former injuries.

However, no matter what specialization is practiced in the way of pre-season training, it is a fact that regularity is the keynote of all training charts—regular sleep, regular meals, regular exercise. This moderate health program allows the basketball player to "hit the books" and get ahead in his work, so that when the season starts he has a head start academically.

Part of the education of an athlete is acquired on the game trips he makes to other sections of the country. He is given excused cuts, but he is still responsible for his classroom work. The pre-season is the time to get a running start on this score. However, if he has any spare time for the basketball court, he should spend it in shooting. This skill cannot be overpracticed. Great players, particularly great shooters, acquire their superior ability in the off-season by constant practice.

TRAINING

SEASON TRAINING

The same rules mentioned in pre-season training apply during the season, namely regular sleep and regular meals. Practice and actual competition will take care of the regular exercise. The players should have a balanced diet except for the day of a game. On the day of a game most coaches are careful to space breakfast, lunch, and dinner properly in order to prevent overloading within a short period. Most coaches try to have the training table pre-game meal four or four and a half hours before game time. This is to ensure proper digestion. The menu for such a meal is usually:

> *Fruit cup*
> *Steak or beef (no gravy)*
> *Carrots and peas, lettuce*
> *Crisp toast (melba or zwieback)*
> *Hot tea*

Although most coaches permit the team a certain amount of freedom on the day of a game, all seem to agree that after the training table the players should go to their rooms and rest until game time. This is for the psychological value if nothing else. Well-meaning friends and strangers should be put off until after the game.

THE TRAINER

There is nothing better than a good trainer, and nothing worse than a bad one. He can make or ruin your team and you'll never know what's happening. The trainer must be the liaison between the player and the coach. He should be a half-mother to the boys, taping them, treating their injuries, and gaining their confidence. Once having this confidence, he'll learn their innermost thoughts. These, properly evaluated, in turn make for a better work relationship between the team and coach. Certainly the trainer must treat all the players alike, being careful not to make pets out of some and pots out of others. That is something he must guard against constantly.

The trainer must be judicious and report what he thinks is important to his coach, and not bother him with petty wailings. A little applied psychology on the part of the trainer is quite often worth all the taping technique in the world. In the world of athletics there are wonderful trainers who have a real love for sports and the boys under their care. They are genuinely interested in each boy as an individual. And what they as trainers lack in technical knowledge of the "basket weave" or the "picnic twist" they more than compensate for in loyalty and real interest in the players and their work. They really feel as bad as the coach when the team loses. A good trainer is worth his weight in gold, which he seldom if ever gets.

Injuries

Just a passing word about injuries. If there is any doubt about a boy's physical condition, there is one place for him, and that is with the doctor. Send him to a physician posthaste for a proper diagnosis. If you can find a doctor who has been a former athlete and isn't of the coddling type, your problems are solved. No attempt will be made here to discuss various injuries. There are many books written on athletic injuries that handle the subject adequately.

DISCIPLINE

One thing is certain: a coach must be in complete control of his team at all times. He must treat all the players alike as far as favors are concerned in order to maintain proper balance on the squad. The star player deserves no better treatment than the lowliest substitute. The star should and does get his rewards elsewhere. The coach must keep alive the incentive to play on the *first five* and not merely to sit on the bench. I've attempted to do this by evaluating the players each week and issuing complimentary tickets to our games on the basis of where they stand on the squad. For example, the first seven players in ability get three tickets each, the next two in ability two each, and the last two on the squad receive only one ticket each.

To keep this competitive interest alive on the entire squad, I occasionally have passed out questionnaires among the members of the team, asking them to rate their fellow-players according to certain abilities. For example: the ten best players listed in the order of their overall value, then the ten best in defensive ability, in shooting, in screening, in playing under the boards, in play perception, and in passing. On other occasions I've had considerable fun going to a blackboard and having a truth party, marking a master chart with the aid of the players. They grade themselves. Here is a sample chart:

Name	Size	Speed	Set Shot	Foul Shot	Screening
Gola	10	10	4	8	10

Play Perception	Stamina	Passing	Reflexes	Attitude
10	10	10	10	10

Name	Size	Speed	Set Shot	Foul Shot	Screening
O'Hara	6	8	4	8	8

Play Perception	Stamina	Passing	Reflexes	Attitude
10	10	10	10	10

Ten is the coefficient for perfect performance in size, speed, screening, play perception, stamina, passing, reflexes, and attitude. The fours given Gola and O'Hara in this example illustrate fine set shooting. They mean 40 per cent successful set shooting. The eights are fine foul shooting—80 per cent. Screening, play perception, stamina, passing, reflexes, and attitude are marked on the basis of 6 for fair, 8 for good, and 10 for perfect. Gola's perfect score would be 92, while O'Hara, because he is smaller and not so fast, suffered only in the marks under the size, speed, and screening columns. He gets a score of 84. If you mark a few and then have the team call out the numbers in unison with you leading the way, you can have fun and at the same time accent elements of good technique. We had a playboy on our team I would purposely mark high in the stamina column just to hear the chorus of boos. Then, I'd settle for a 6.

If you have properly screened the boys before they entered college there will be few disciplinary problems. Boys want to play basketball and one way to punish them is to not let them play for awhile. For some particularly bad act, cutting them from the squad for several days is about the most severe thing I've ever been forced to do.

I recall one incident that might be of interest. One of my young sophomore players, of whom I expected great things and who has since justified that feeling, didn't realize the importance of mastering an outside set shot. After he had played several games in his sophomore year, the scouts indicated that he wouldn't and couldn't shoot outside. Opponents began to drop off him and we were unable to get into the basket. Finally, I had to bench him, since he wouldn't listen to my instructions to bone up on his set shooting. With another outside shooter in, we began to win again. The sophomore was quite disconsolate sitting on the bench. He tried to alibi his inaction by sitting there with a taped knee. Finally, running out of reasons to tell his friends, he approached me with the following: "Coach, I hear you're saying behind my back that I've been drinking."

I replied that I hadn't said anything to anyone but, now that he had mentioned it, I'd tell him. "On your way home tonight," I said, "go into a bar and drink as much liquor as you can afford. Do the same thing on your way to practice tomorrow. But when you get here practice set shots if you can still stand up. When you can make the set shot you'll play again."

He looked at me in amazement, slightly taken back. The next thing I knew he was practicing set shots and went on to become one of the stars in the national championship game with his magnificent outside shooting. I offer this for what it may be worth in having boys face up to the facts. It has been my experience that, if the coach is completely honest with the players, there will be a minimum of disciplinary problems.

PRACTICE

Practice sessions vary according to the school. I found that sessions of more than an hour and a half tend to kill the interest of the players. *Send them away from practice wanting a little more.* Who is it said, "Get up from the table a little hungry."?

Half an hour on set shooting at the start of practice, half an hour or more on generalized offense, and half an hour on specialized defense and offense seem to be a good working schedule. (See Diagrams 10 through 15, pages 54, 63–65.) The day before the game is divided between foul and set shooting, working against specialized zone defenses, and any other specialized patterns the scouting report shows we can expect during the game.

It also is desirable to spend some time on movie instruction, if films of games are available. I know of no better way to teach defense than by movies. Players will resist your evaluation and criticism of their play and even deny certain acts, until they are shown on film. The use of films is predicated on the size of your basketball budget, which ordinarily isn't large enough except in big basketball schools. But the value of movies cannot be contested.

Players should be made to dress with adjoining lockers and not away from each other. In that way there is no opportunity to carry on grudges that might arise out of competition during practices. If you are thrown in with a man, you either square your differences or forget them. You fight or shut up. Then too, the dressing room of the players should rarely if ever be invaded by the coach. They should have some place to let off steam after a hard workout. They should be given that opportunity in their own privacy. It will relieve their tension and they'll be ready to go the next day.

Make no mistake, coaching a top-flight basketball team is no pink tea. The necessity for excessive drill so that individuals can be molded into a team thinking process is a real chore. There is no time for little niceties that will get you the reward as the "most popular and sweetest man who ever coached us." If you receive that award, it more often than not will be from a last-place team. You as the coach must dominate the play thinking until the team thinks as one person. You eliminate individualists and in so doing rub personalities. The time for sweetness and light is after the season is finished and the war is won, or at least fought to the utmost of your ability. That is the very purpose of competitive athletics. If you don't intend to put forth your best effort as a coach or player, then better you be in intramural sports or "bowling on the green."

Merely being severe is not enough. I've known coaches who were severe but not specific and constructive in their criticisms. Boys will break their necks doing what you want them to do if you know your stuff. They'll yawn if you don't, and rightly so.

To get the job done I don't think any coach can get away with cursing the players. You must have a whip in your voice but this can be accomplished without profanity, by means of sarcastic references or other subtle methods. What serves as a lash is an individual matter. The personality involved must be taken into consideration. You handle each boy differently. Some need to be told, others needled. Those differences are what makes coaching a fascinating profession.

THE MANAGER

A good manager is very important. He can take a number of burdensome details from the coach's shoulders. Of course, the coach has to be wise enough to delegate authority to the manager. Many coaches I know give the impression of being overworked and harrassed, which they are, but only because they try to take care of every little detail themselves. A real coach should give the manager duties that will make the manager feel he is more than an errand boy. Actually, a top-flight student manager, properly trained as an assistant for at least two years, can take care of all the business details. He can handle transportation arrangements and hotel accommodations on trips. And he can take care of the complimentary ticket job.

One of the manager's most important jobs is acting as a scorer at the official table. He is our check on the official scorer and, if he sees anything that doesn't look right, it's his job to call it to the attention of the officials. I know one manager who caught the official timekeeper, a student of the home college, allowing the clock to run in the late minutes of the game when the home team was ahead and fouls were being shot. This manager was alert to the fact that the clock is not supposed to run until the foul has been shot. His alertness in calling the timer's action to the attention of the officials helped his team win a game it might have lost.

It is a sorry spectacle to see an athletic director or coach rushing about before a game like a mother hen, taking care of details that could and should be handled by an 18-year-old. If you can't trust the manager, get rid of him and establish some competitive system whereby the efficient man will work up to the top. Then you won't have to worry. He'll have what it takes. A manager usually has three or four assistants who vie for the right to be manager-elect. Most colleges give the varsity manager a regular varsity letter and therefore should give him responsibilities that make him worthy of that monogram.

Post-season

After a grueling basketball season the players should taper off from training gradually. Ordinarily this doesn't present much of a problem because basketball players usually are baseball players also, and the change to a slower game takes care of this tapering off process. It is recommended, however, that some spring sport be played at an intramural level just to keep the body processes in order. Stopping all exercise is certainly not the best thing to do. As a practical matter, good basketball players—lovers of the game—continue to play casually with the approval of the proper authorities. It is surprising that some boys play the game all year round.

8

PRE-GAME TACTICS

THERE ARE TWO IMPORTANT THINGS TO BE CONsidered in preparing your team to meet an opponent: (1) what the opponent has done in the past—information obtained from scouting reports, and (2) what the opposition will do against your team. You arrive at the latter by putting yourself in the position of the opponents. In other words, what would you do against your own team were you playing them?

SCOUTING REPORTS

Scouting reports can be of great, some, or little value, according to who makes them. I have read scouting reports that describe everything from the girl friend of the star player to the color shoe he is wearing—a veritable mass of unimportant information. The best information should be obtained by the coach personally scouting the opposition or by his having one of his former players scout them. The coach or former player knows what pertinent information to look for that will be of value to their particular style of play.

Let's pass over the voluminous masses of unimportant information and go to some of the things that a coach would like to know about an opponent. His first question is: "What are the shooting habits of the opponents?" He wants to know where certain individuals shoot from best, where most of the team shooting is done from, what type of shots are most often taken, and whether the shots are taken as the result of a quick break, from behind a screen, or are just ordinary set or jump shots. In which direction do the individual shooters go before they shoot? Once having possession of the ball, do the players always shoot, or will they occasionally pass off to a teammate? What type defense was being employed against the opponent at the time the shot chart was made? Where was the scoring done from when a zone was used? When a man-for-man defense was used? Nearly all this information can be gleamed from a properly recorded shot chart.

The next factor a good scouting report should cover is the size and speed of the opponents. Can they be matched man for man in size and speed? Will matching for size bring about inequalities in speed? Will the opponents employ their speed up and down the court, or will they permit time for a set defense? What is the size, speed, and shooting strength of the substitutes most likely to see action? Will the use of a substitute vary the opponents' attack? In the event that physical matching of the opponents isn't possible, is a type of zone desirable?

Assuming that the opponents cannot be matched

man for man physically, what type of zone will be most effective against them? Should it be a constant zone or should it be an occasional zone? Do the opponents readily realize when they are being zoned, or do they continue to operate oblivious of this fact?

What style of offense do they use: set play or continuity? What happens when the defensive man plays in front of the pivot man? Do the outside feeders change position when the ball is thrown to the pivot man? When the man is in the pivot, are the corners occupied by offensive men? What kind of out-of-bounds plays do they use? Where do they tip the ball in held-ball situations? How do they line up when jumping in held-ball situations that they don't control? Does a press defense unbalance them? Do key men foul excessively or tire quickly? Are certain players poor foul-shooters? Will they pace themselves as a team during the game, and will they have balance between the offense and defense?

These are some of the questions coaches would like to have answered by a scout or scouting report. Now, having the information is one thing; doing something about it is another. A coach should know the capabilities of his team and realize what he can and cannot do. There is a danger in getting too complicated in the diagnosis. A famous lawyer once said there is always a variance "between the *allegata* and the *probata*": between what you try to prove and what you really prove. So try not to overburden your team with scouting information.

Mental Attitude

The day has long since passed when coaches could walk into a dressing room and spellbind a team into heroic action beyond their natural abilities. Stories constantly are told about such achievements, but generally they are the product of some sportswriter's imagination or of some coach's wishful thinking. The modern boy can't be fooled anymore as we possibly were in the "good old days." Maybe the old idea of "Die for dear old Siwash" was a good thing, and we might do well to return to a little of the same. But by and large the average youth has a healthy viewpoint of competitive sports.

However, I do remember one time when a coach pulled all the stops in a very short but pertinent pre-game speech. It had a definite effect on his team's attitude. Bradley Tech, national champion the year previous, was sitting in the dressing room next to the one occupied by the small Yale team I was coaching. The rooms were separated by a thin partition. My players were sitting quietly awaiting a few words on tactics, when through the thin partition boomed the voice of the Bradley Tech coach. "Seated in the next room," said the Bradley coach to his team, "are the boys whose fathers own the factories you will work in the rest of your lives. But you're not working for them *tonight*—OR ARE YOU?" I don't have to mention that Bradley walloped Yale, maybe even more soundly than they would have had the pep talk not been given.

I have always tried to be factual about pre-game

situations.   I'm of the opinion that last-minute imploring and volcanic outbursts of emotion never really solve many tactical problems.   If the coach has been completely honest with his team and has not tried to boost them up synthetically at other times, their attitude is generally satisfactory.   Victory generally comes to the team that remembers the scouting information, is physically fit to compete, and also has a true estimate and respect for the opponents' ability.   Someplace between the phony dirges of "We won't score a first down" to "We'll murder the bums" is a middle-ground that is usually the healthiest frame of mind for a team—a realization that the job will be hard but it can be done.

In recent years my LaSalle teams often have been described as having a cold, professional air about them. That air has persisted after the game, with an inner glow that comes from a job sensibly and well done but with little of the outward exuberance that comes from a surprising windfall from heaven.   Those boys prepared carefully and laboriously for their triumphs and felt they were the natural outcome of that planning.   After they had won the national championships (NCAA and NIT), photographers had to tell them, "Jump up and down and make like you were happy."   They *were* happy, but inside.   And if they hadn't won maybe we could have taken comfort from that poem by Edgar A. Guest, "What Makes the Game":*

---

* "What Makes the Game" is from the book, *Life's Highway*, by Edgar A. Guest, Copyright 1933, The Reilly & Lee Co., Chicago, Illinois.

"I fumbled," said the sad-eyed lad,
"And lost the golden chance I had!"
"That's quite all right," his coach replied,
"I understand how hard you tried.
Forget it now.   Go back and fight
With all your strength and all your might.

"Take hold of this consoling thought:
If every ball that's thrown were caught;
If no one faltered; no one fell;
If every play we tried went well;
If gain with every venture came,
There would be nothing to the game.

"What makes the game?   Not perfect play,
But golden chances thrown away!
The fumbled ball; the slight mistake
Which men however skillful make,
The faulty judgment and the will
To wait and work for victory still.

"And so with life!   If all were plain:
If men perfection could attain,
If neither doubt nor loss nor fear
Should ever test our courage here;
If we knew all, and all could see,
Then deadly dull this life would be.

9

GAME TACTICS

I RECENTLY MET A COACH OF A LARGE UNIVERSITY shortly before my team was due to take the floor for a championship game. He came up with the following remark: "Ken, I figure that on the night of a game it is too late to do much about anything. So I take myself a couple of good slugs of liquor before I go to the gym and let the chips fall where they may."

I shouldn't have to say that every other basketball coach I've talked with thoroughly disagrees with this philosophy. I feel, and I've coached most sports, that the basketball coach is closer to, more a part of—and either an aid or a detriment to his team to a greater degree—than the coach of any other sport. I hope I'm able to convince you readers of this, if only to evoke a little sympathy and understanding for the coach, be he high school, college, or professional. His real reward is a feeling of satisfaction for an intricate job well done; and that comes from within. Few can or care to see the minute turns of fate that determine victory or defeat. Let's try to point out some of these, if only to increase your watching interest at the next game you attend.

Let's go to the scene of the game: the gymnasium. You should time your arrival at the gym, if possible, to avoid players loitering in the lobby, talking to friends who tend to take their minds off the game. The curse of trying to get last-minute free tickets for well-meaning friends is a cancer on the body of the American sporting scene. Those are managerial problems that should be handled by the manager. Then too, with the recent basketball point-shaving scandals still ringing in his ears, the careful coach is suspicious of every individual he sees talking to his men.

Maybe I have been overly suspicious, but my care and interest on the day of a game once gave rise to a laughable incident. This happened about six years ago when I took my first LaSalle team to play North Carolina State at Raleigh. We were staying at a hotel that faced a park. On the afternoon of the game I came upon my center, the now famous Larry Foust, talking with what seemed to me to be an overly prosperous looking individual who looked to my pre-game mind like a city slicker.

I walked over to Larry and called him aside. "Who is that fellow you're talking to?" I asked him. Foust told me it was Buck Freeman, a famous athlete in his day who was scouting for Coach Frank McGuire of St. John's College (Brooklyn). Freeman now is assistant coach to McGuire at the University of North Carolina. I had heard of Buck but had never met him, and I jumped at the conclusion that a guy as well dressed as that just couldn't be a coach or a plain fan.

Assuming that the scouting information has been gone over in previous practices, at the pre-game meal, or at a meeting called for that purpose on the day of the game, there is very little need for much talking in the dressing room. There should be a quiet, calm atmosphere in the room. The boys should realize that they have a tough job ahead of them and that they have to attack it according to our carefully laid plans.

If the tension is too great it might be well for the coach, or someone else whose humor is equally corny, to make with a joke that has nothing to do with the game. I recall one that relaxed a team that needed no relaxing, but rather more and better players. I had an undermanned Yale team at Hanover, New Hampshire, to play Dartmouth in the Winter Carnival game. "Ossie" Cowells had another great Dartmouth team, that included the talented Broberg. We were sitting in the dressing room when a telegram was delivered addressed to me. I must mention first that the names of three of my players were Rhett, Bartholomy, and Owen—all great guys but slightly inexperienced and hardly big enough by modern basketball standards. They did have wonderful senses of humor, however. I opened the telegram, which read, "Good luck in tonight's game, especially to Rhett, Bartholomy, and Owen. (signed) Rhett, Bartholomy, and Owen."

We go over the dominant features of our attack in the dressing room, probably matching men and touching on the type of tip-off play we will use. Then, with the usual words of "Let's go down and see what happens," we leave for the floor. "Let's see what happens" means we expect to have new developments in the game that will call for tactical adjustments during time-out periods and at half-time.

We have quite often felt out the opponent in the first quarter, tried several defenses in the second quarter, evaluated these experiences between halves, won the game in the third period, and then held on to this lead until the end. That, in my mind, is good game technique, but I'm getting the game over too fast.

Before starting the game, a word about warmup exercises. I have been asked quite often for types of warmup drills. There are two types of drills: (*1*) those that look fancy but bear no relation to the maneuvers that will occur in the game, and (*2*) drills that duplicate game-playing situations. When I was coaching in the pro league, where a game is a show in addition to a contest, we had a lot of tricky passing in our warmup drills. In college competition, however, we occupy ourselves with skills that are part of our overall weave-screen flash-pivot offense. In other words, we practice weaving a little in several drills and working the flash pivot in another drill, and then we drop out of the moving drills to complete the pre-game warmup with set and foul shooting.

Now to the game itself. The ball is tossed up at center and you, the coach, are playing it in your own mind. You watch the movements of all your players and have an assistant look at certain things done by the opponents. You know that, if your boys are doing things correctly, you can forget about the opponents. The ball is thrown up at center and you've learned something already. Your best jumper at center had been decisively outjumped by his opponent. That may and generally does mean that you won't dominate the play off the backboards, at least where those two boys are concerned. A case in point occurred in the Bradley-LaSalle championship game in 1954. Gola was outjumped by his opponent at the beginning of the game and at the half. That was one of several reasons we had for playing Gola on the outside that night, a decision which my critics—my first-half critics anyway—had a field day with.

Since the game no longer is played in quarters, a time-out should be taken halfway through the first half in order to have a little confab on the weaknesses of the opponents as observed by both the players and you from the sidelines. I have made it a habit to seat my players in front of me during time-outs. While the trainer wipes them with wet, cool towels, we trade information and diagnose. The following might be some of the questions that would have to be resolved:

(*1*) Who can outboard his man?

(*2*) Who can give and go on his man?

(*3*) How is your man playing you on the baseline? Will he let you go two ways? Can you get into the pivot?

(*4*) Who is faster than who?

(*5*) Whom on the opposition must we double-team?

(*6*) Can we overplay certain men to the right or left?

(*7*) What does their pivot man do when we play in front of him? Do the outside back-court feeders change position after they have thrown the ball into the pivot?

(*8*) Does the defense drop back quickly and completely?

(*9*) Are we controlling the boards or just the defensive one?

Certainly all these questions are not resolved in the short time-out period. But the experienced coach can cut through these questions and arrive at the ones that are causing trouble. He will be able to quickly mend and adjust. One failure to adjust quickly and several points that might mean the difference between victory and defeat can be scored.

Let's move on to the final ten minutes of the first half. If you have the upper hand both offensively and defensively, the only reason for substituting would be to rest your starters. We avoid this though, since in the screen-weave flash-pivot offense players can go into pivot-shuttling positions in the four-one, three-two attacks previously discussed. You will recall the statement that you REST ON OFFENSE AND WORK ON DEFENSE. Well, you may, if you are not completely in control of the game, try several styles of zones in order to get the offensive reaction to them. If one is effective it might be well to drop it and then come back with it in the second half, when your opponent has not had the opportunity to diagnose it.

Or, if an opponent is exhibiting a defensive weakness, you should not exploit it until the latter stages of the game. Otherwise the opposing coach will get his weak man out of there and this opportunity for an easy score may be lost. We purposely have stayed away from certain opponents so they wouldn't foul out. It was our feeling that the opposition was weaker with him in there than with a substitute who might have certain abilities we would not be able to contend with so well.

One thing is certain: don't waste your time-outs in the early stages of the game. Save them for the critical late-game periods, when matters of strategy must be talked over and planned. This fact was brought home to me in an NCAA play-off game against Fordham. I'll tell you about that game later in a further discussion on tactics.

HALF-TIME EVALUATION

I have found it helpful to crystallize my thoughts on the happenings of the first half while casually and slowly making my way to the dressing room. The trainer will be busy with the players, wiping them off with towels, adjusting any tape that may have come loose, and ministering to any injuries that may have been incurred. The trainer's chores take approximately five of the fifteen minutes allotted between halves. When the players are calmed and sitting down it is time to rediagnose the opposition collectively and individually. During the first half I generally have someone taking notes on the mistakes we have made. I use these as the basis for my criticism or praise, whichever may be in order.

The coach should learn in the first half which of his men are faster than their opponents, which ones are switching men, which men are best on the defensive and offensive boards, which are the poorest and strongest defensive men, which men are shooting best and most. He should know by this time the most effective zone used and the one being held back as a surprise maneuver. The latter should have been devised from the scouting report on the opponent.

You should examine the scorebook and learn how many opponents are in danger of fouling out of the game. If they are strong opponents you should direct your attack and drive-ins at them, inviting them to foul again. If they are weak opponents you want to keep them in the game and don't necessarily direct your attack at them. You may decide to let one of your regulars sit out part of the second half to give him a sideline look at something that is happening and which he will have a better understanding of after he has seen it from the bench. Watching without being occupied with playing a man quite often gives a player a better view of his relation to the whole offensive or defensive plan.

All of this has to be done in the short space of about seven minutes, with each player being given an opportunity to express his personal reaction to certain players. The coach, of course, must make the final and conclusive decision on the tactics to be used in the second half. So back to the playing floor we go for three minutes of practice shooting on particular shots missed in the first half.

All things being equal, and if you have made a correct diagnosis, your team should go into the lead during the third period, particularly early in the third period. All things being equal again, and since the opponents also have spent the half-time rest diagnosing *your* movements, victory will go to the team with the best diagnosticians. Herein lies the fascination of coaching. The coach who experiences the thrill of having his team execute his plan, in the third quarter after a half-time diagnosis, has lived, although the great number of fans will never know it, or admit it if they do know it.

If you have a firm lead going into the latter part of the game, the offense should be reduced in tempo. More careful shots should be taken with more ball handling for more certainty. It's just like a fighter who is way ahead on points in the ninth round. He won't expose his chin. The decision to gamble rests with the losing team or the losing man. Slowing down the offense with a long pivot and with give and go's has been suggested as one method of protecting a lead. Many, however, will decry this, although I have always felt that, if a team is good enough to be ahead at the three-quarter mark, it deserves the advantage of making the other fellow play its game. Tomorrow night the shoe may be on the other foot.

A change of team pace is just another of those variations in tactics and techniques that make basketball such an interesting sport to watch. But you have to know what to look for.

The reader might be interested in two game situations that illustrate the effectiveness of planned tactics. One occurred in the Bradley-LaSalle game for the 1954 NCAA title at Kansas City. Bradley in the early stages of the game dominated the play. Unable to stop Bradley with a standard man-to-man defense, LaSalle tried a switching and then a one-three-one zone, neither of which was successful. When LaSalle was in the one-three-one zone (which has corner weaknesses) Bradley scored at will from the corners.

It was apparent, with five minutes to go before half-time, that neither of the previous defenses was the answer to the Bradley offense. A new defense had to be used that would give defensive strength in the corners. We decided on a shuttling two-three zone, but did not use it in the first half since we didn't want to give the Bradley coach a chance to evaluate it during the intermission. The element of surprise in the second half would have been gone. The second half is basketball history. LaSalle ran up a big enough lead in the early minutes of the final half to score a decisive victory. The shoe has been on the other foot at other times. We have lost games when opposing coaches surprised me with a new look defense at the start of the second half. Sometimes you win and sometimes you lose.

The other situation illustrative of game tactics arose on the Fordham-LaSalle play-off game in Buffalo, New York the same year. Each team was fighting to remain in the NCAA Tournament. LaSalle had beaten Fordham decisively earlier in the season. But Fordham had a great team ably coached by John Bach, and I knew they would be tough to beat the second time. Nothing could have been truer, for with ten seconds to go the game was tied with Fordham in possession of the ball maneuvering for a last shot. They took a shot and, although they missed the rebound, the ball came into the hands of a Fordham player who scored.

Frank O'Hara, our captain, called time-out with five seconds to play. We had the ball at our defensive baseline. Ordinarily it would take that long to get the ball to the front court alone. We huddled at the bench and arranged to take an immediate time-out upon throwing the ball in. When the ball was thrown in all of us called time-out. The ball now was at mid-court with four seconds to go. We then set up a play with Tom Gola in the left-hand deep baseline offensive corner, Charley Singley and Fran O'Malley under the offensive basket, O'Hara throwing the ball in, and Charley Greenberg driving to Gola for screening purposes. When play was resumed Gola came out of the corner behind Greenberg's screen. O'Hara hit Gola at the foul line. O'Malley's man left him to help out on Gola, who then passed to O'Malley under the basket for the tying goal as the buzzer sounded. Buffalo fans say it was the greatest play series they have ever seen and the execution was particularly pleasing to me. We won the game in overtime and went on to win the national title.

I would be remiss in this book if I didn't pay my respects to all the substitutes who never quite get the credit due them. The world may say that it isn't interested in who finishes second, but the real coach knows that his team quite often finishes first because it has been paced and pressed by the substitute day after day and week after week. Their reward—to sit and hope and sit some more. They are the understudies, as in the theatre, hoping that the play will go well, but at the same time hoping for a chance to act themselves. Let me then pay my respects to all the second team players I've coached in all these years, with a verse from the poem entitled "The Crate."

> Vain is the skill of workmen great—
> Unless the boy who makes the crate
> Shall do his best at driving nails,

The work of all the others fails.
There is no unimportant task—
Whatever duty life may ask,
On it depends another plan;
There is no unimportant man.*

* "The Crate," by Edgar A. Guest, is reprinted by permission of the Reilly & Lee Co., Chicago, Illinois.

10

POST-GAME

PROCEDURE

EVERY COACH WILL HAVE HIS OWN POST-GAME PRO-
cedure and it will vary according to the personnel on
the team. No two teams are alike. Teams vary as individuals do. Coaching attitudes will vary from the
approach of a mother hen to that of a completely grown-
up demeanor. I believe the mother hen method is quite
ludicrous to the modern youth who doesn't seem to want
to be mothered. I believe in treating my players like
men until they prove themselves otherwise.

Here are a few rules I might pass on as at least food
for thought. I have tried generally to adopt the attitude
that the players are college men and responsible individuals who don't have to be fawned over. Individuals
do alter methods and sometimes a slight adjustment is
called for. But on to post-game procedure. I've
learned these things from sad experience:

(1) Make your entries into the dressing room after winning and losing as nearly alike as possible. I merely announce the time of the next practice if we've lost, and set the hour of curfew, and the time to get up and leave if we are traveling. It will be time enough after I've slept on the mistakes to discuss them. If you've won, a simple "Good game" should be enough. The newspapers and all the players' friends will have them in the clouds. You have to ready them for the next game. It's time enough after the season is over to go into ecstasy over good performance. I've seen teams that varied from game to game like day and night, partly because their coaches were so lavish in their praise after a win. It took a defeat to bring these clubs down out of the clouds and back to earth. Praise is a wonderful and dangerous weapon and should be handled like rare wine—carefully.

(2) Keep your dressing room free of people who have no business connection with the team. Players after a tough game are liable to say anything, including things they don't mean or that sound different than they were really intended. Good teams, like good race horses, are high strung, and their statements are apt to be exaggerated and misunderstood by people not used to being around athletes. They say griping armies are the best armies.

(3) If possible, try to stay away from all but your most

intimate and understanding friends after the game. If you smile your enemies will say you are taking the game too lightly. If you don't smile they say you can't take it and don't accept defeat gracefully enough. In short, you can't win.

(4) My experience with the press is mingled. They can help you or hurt you, and I'll dismiss this topic with the observation that they certainly must be reckoned with. The right kind of write-up before a game can help immeasurably in killing overconfidence. The right kind of a story can often pick a beaten team up off the floor. There is something about the printed word that lends force to its meaning.

It's too bad that such a weapon sometimes is in the hands of the malicious, the frustrated, and the critically unfair and immature. There are great and good writers and they are a joy forever. They don't have to praise the coach to earn that description. They merely have to be discerning and fair in their approach to the sport. It is a game played by young fellows, not necessarily by perfectionists. I'm talking about college and school players, of course. Many of my most endearing and critical friends are reporters.

Exhaust every means within the rules to win, and hurt a little if you don't. But remember, like baseball, it's still a game that, in the words of Red Smith, "little boys can play."

☆ **11**

SCHEDULES

WHEN THE LATE ALBERT EINSTEIN EVOLVED HIS theory of relativity he could have had in mind the making of athletic schedules. The theory of relativity most certainly comes in for practical application in schedule making. As the minor league baseball player knocks the stuffing out of the ball, only to falter miserably in the big leagues, so can college basketball teams be terrific against minor opposition and ordinary against major opponents. Victory is relative. Take Kentucky for example. Many coaches feel that Kentucky has been piling up its great record in a "pony league" where the opposition has been relatively weak. If this has been true things may change from now on. For Alabama, Georgia Tech, and several others in the Southeast Conference are beginning to take the game more seriously. And the bulky, balding Baron himself admits that things could be tough from now on.

Any great team can lose often if it plays among the tough independents away from home. Any good team in the past few years that has taken on Duquesne, Holy

Cross, Seton Hall, or LaSalle could have got itself licked as often as not. And it is to the eternal credit of some of my LaSalle boys that they have amassed a splendid record in the past six years against all comers. LaSalle had one of the best road-winning percentages of any team in the nation. And we traveled from coast to coast.

There was a time when athletic directors made basketball schedules with breathers at the beginning of the season and traditional rivals at the end. Harvard and Yale still try to do this, feeling that the success or failure of a season rests on the outcome of this heated New England rivalry. I don't know whether it's still the case or not, but at one time a Yale or Harvard boy could earn his varsity letter only if he played in the Harvard-Yale game. This was true, not only in basketball, but in all sports between these two Ivy League rivals. As a result of this custom—should I say common law, which is crystallized custom?—both coaches would send in their substitutes at the same time so that neither team was too badly hurt by "earn-your-letter reserves."

Be that as it may, it still is highly desirable to play against key rivals near the end of the season, if for no other reason than to keep up the interest of the players who might be experiencing a bad season against other opponents. Hope in that way springs eternal, even in the hardened heart of the coach who, in a losing season, is the loneliest man in town.

The story is told that Hank Iba, when he first

started coaching, took many a defeat at the University of Colorado because he didn't have a big man who could get the ball off the boards. He came home rather despondent one night and sat down to think things over. His wife remarked, "Hank, you may as well face it. You've got to get yourself a big boy." Henry looked up and said soulfully, "And now even you are against me." But he must have heeded her advice, for not too long later Hank showed up at Oklahoma A. & M. with a seven-foot kid named Bob Kurland. The outcome of this association is history and Hank wasn't lonely for a long time after.

The tremendous growth in the popularity of basketball all over the world has brought athletic directors a new headache—tournament games, both holiday and post-season. Most college teams play about 25 games, which averages about two a week. This allows proper time for game preparation and studies. The holiday tournaments are so well liked by both the boys and the athletic directors—they help balance the budget—that sometimes less regular games are scheduled to fit in with the tournaments. In other words, sometimes the schedule has to be built around the tournament dates, if you're lucky enough to be invited.

Each of the teams that played in the well-run Kentucky Tournament in 1954 took home $10,000 for playing two games. If in addition a college is able to participate in a post-season tourney and make the finals, it is possible to pick up a check for another $7,000.

Little wonder that small schools in particular accent basketball.

Another desirable feature of schedules is an opportunity for your boys to play teams away from home. Someone has said that travel is broadening. They're right. The players do like trips. For many it is the first time they have ever been in a pullman car, a hotel, or a plane. Then too traveling affords them an opportunity to meet new people in other sections of the country. One of the purposes of a higher education is to make the students well-rounded individuals. Travel helps. Who was it who said, "Send your son to college and the boys will educate him"? Let's add, "Send your son to college and out for a team and the boys and the travel will educate him."

Listening in on athletic directors discussing their schedule problems, it would appear that the ultimate salvation of all colleges from a scheduling standpoint would be the formation of leagues. The independent schools without league affiliations find that, if they have good teams, no one wants to schedule them. If they're bad everyone wants to play them, unless they're so bad the gate will suffer. League teams, theoretically, meet on an equal basis in the matter of scholastic requirements, grants in aid, and facilities. They allegedly are bound by uniform rules that are supposed to make the competition even. This is as it should be. You plan your league schedule, work in a few intersectional and sectional rivals, and the schedule is complete.

SCHEDULES

Leagues are a good thing too from the standpoint of building up student interest in your team. League records are kept both individually and collectively. You shoot for those records. Even a losing team in a league can maintain the interest of its followers with perhaps an individual's shooting for a scoring championship or a big upset over the league leaders. More traditional rivalries are built up in leagues.

It might be well to mention at this time that the five colleges in the Philadelphia Area, Penn, Temple, Villanova, St. Joseph's, and LaSalle, now are playing basketball on the same court in doubleheader partnership. Three doubleheaders a week—Wednesday, Friday and Saturday night—are scheduled, with the teams playing intersectional opponents, sectional rivals, and each other in a city series. This should increase the interest in college basketball in Philadelphia. Almost everyone expected difficulty when the joint master schedule had to be worked out. But surprisingly it was prepared in short order—a credit to all the athletic directors concerned. The directors are all former athletes of greater or lesser stature. Maybe they remembered their lessons of team play and give and take. Or could it be that they don't have to coach a team?

It might be well to touch on one evil that can come up in scheduling—over-scheduling. Smart coaches and athletic directors should cooperate in scheduling according to the material available, and according to the strength of the team if at all possible. I don't mean that the team should be under-scheduled and win all of its games against the much maligned "Little Sisters of the Poor." But going to the other extreme and allowing your team to be trounced repeatedly isn't good either.

The late Jock Sutherland once said he never wanted to put a team on the field that didn't have a chance to win. He felt, as all of us feel, that repeated trouncings defeat the purpose of the game and the spirit of the boys. It's nice to win some of the time and to get your share of victories. Herman Hickman, upon taking the job as Yale football coach, said he hoped to win enough to keep the alumni sullen but not mutinous. Captain Bligh of the good ship *Bounty* could have told him it becomes rather difficult to maintain that balance. Tad Wieman, the old Princeton coach, once said, "Win just about half your games. Then the alumni won't be quite sure whether it's your fault or the material's. And never win a championship, or the next year they'll expect it."

So a word to young coaches. Schedule carefully, with balance if possible. And if you don't happen to be your own athletic director like Eddie Hickey, Hank Iba, and others, be as close to your athletic director as Damon was to Pythias. The price of liberty is eternal vigilance. On the other hand, don't play so many "Little Sisters of the Poor" that your team will relax and won't be ready for the big ones, the "Big Brothers of the Rich."

Just as the Harlem Globetrotters excited the first interest in basketball in many places, it might also be said that the various press polls determining the top ten teams have kept the interest in basketball at a weekly fever pitch once the season has started. Although they are, in my opinion, no more accurate than the evaluation of a man's reputation as distinct from his character— since your character is what you really are and your reputation is what people think you are—they do serve to promote discussion and interest.

Sectionalism brings about a united vote for one particular team that might be playing a comparatively weak schedule. In one service poll, coaches doing the voting might not like other coaches and might vote them down or up as the case may be. However, I believe that by the end of the season the first ten or twenty in the country have emerged. The cream has a way of coming to the top. And I suppose on a given night any one of these teams could defeat the other. That's what makes horse racing. Teams try hard to hold and improve their rankings, since the top teams usually wind up in post-season tournaments. The tournament selection committees seem to be guided by the national rankings. Let's dismiss these polls then with the simple statement that they are good because they stimulate overall basketball interest. Let's take them as a girl takes a dilettante lover: interesting, entertaining, but not to be taken seriously.

☆ **12**

OFFICIATING AND RULES

(WITH APOLOGIES TO NO ONE BUT JOYCE KILMER, author of "Trees"):

> I think that I shall never see
> A satisfactory referee,
> About whose head a halo shines,
> Whose merit rates reporters' lines,
> One who calls them as they are,
> And not as I would wish by far.
>
> A gent who leans not either way,
> But lets the boys decide the play,
> A man who knows the rules by heart,
> And uses judgment from the start.
> Poems are made by fools like me,
> But only God could referee.

With that poetic observation and the further

observation that I have had two rhubarbs of world magnitude with a total of two officials in 25 years of coaching, let's go on to further discussion of this always controversial phase of basketball.

There are two major weaknesses of the game of basketball: (*1*) the excessive influence that poor officiating can have on the game and on its outcome and (*2*) the tremendous advantage that the excessively large man has over the smaller man. The speed of the game calls for the exercise of judgment in so many fast developing situations that the job of the basketball official is a herculean one if properly performed. Coaches realize the difficulty of the job, since most of us have officiated at one time or another. And coaches will agree that the one unforgivable sin in an official is to call a play that he is not in a position to see properly. The second and more rarely occurring sin is for an official to lean one way or the other. I have only experienced what I thought was leaning twice in my 25-year association with basketball. I think that is a compliment to officials in general. (See Illustration 32 on page 99.)

We coaches by and large have no quarrel with poor officials, as long as they are consistently poor both ways. An official can't help it if he has bad judgment. Coaches quite often are born that way too. And coaches can even forgive an official if he can't get around the court, for this weakness will also balance out. Sometimes you'll be favored because of his disability and sometimes you'll lose by it.

I have toyed with the idea that maybe one official would be enough to call a game. He would call everything he saw. Since he would not see as much as two officials, he at least would be consistently blind and the game would not be spoiled by over-officiating. The old Cleveland Rosenblooms once had an official raised in the air above the middle of the floor. He was the overall judge. He had four held-ball tossers stationed about the floor. I think it worked out pretty well, and at least there weren't two officials trying to outdo each other in calling fouls. We didn't have two inconsistent callers feeling they had to blow once in a while to earn their money.

I do feel that officiating is getting better each year. Greater uniformity is being achieved through clinics for officials and through intersectional officiating. I would like to see movies taken of key games by the rules committee, with a running commentary on the nature of the fouls called and an accompanying clinical discussion of them. Then at the end of the season these movies could be studied by the right parties, from the standpoint of advocating both rule changes and proper officiating. Maybe this system or something like it is being employed, but I doubt it judging from the howl that went up when I suggested I wanted to take movies of one of our games specifically to check the work of an official. I wanted to use the movies in my clinical discussions. The cry of protest could be heard all over the world. Actually, I would welcome movies of my coaching methods, both at game time and during any practice session. "See, Watson, nothing in my sleeves."

Let's look at this problem from the standpoint of the officials. They feel, and rightly so, that some coaches are making goats out of them to alibi their own coaching deficiencies and losses. I'm inclined to agree with them in certain cases. I have coaching colleagues who never lose a game. The officials lose it for them. Every coach disagrees in the course of a game on certain isolated calls. He may even protest. Officials don't mind that, since they understand the pressure the coach is under. I have found I can get across to an official almost any point I want to, as long as I do it without trying to make him look bad to the crowd. The easiest thing to do is to go down near the timer's bench during a time-out and, while looking at the scorekeeper, address the official without looking at him. Tell him what you think is happening. "They're roughing my pivot man," etc. The official doesn't have to pay any attention to you, but at least you get it off your mind without antagonizing him. Who knows, he might even take heed, or at least look twice to see if even a coach could be right.

No coach should want the edge, although I've heard one prominent coach say he wants it at home because he never gets it away from home. He has the advantage at home, surprisingly enough, but he can't win a game away from his own court. Most of the coaches I know merely want two things in an official: complete honesty and a willingness to get into position to call the plays. An official should not call a play he is not in a position to see. I prefer that officials work with their whistles in their hands rather than in their mouths. It makes them less impetuous in their calls. If an official has to take time to get the whistle to his mouth and then blow it, he is doubly sure of an infraction. "Anticipators" who call a foul before it is made seem to be trying to impress people with their quick reactions. I would rather have an interval of deliberation, however momentary. It's much better than the quick, sometimes doubtful call. An official always can recall a play, but when he blows the whistle too quickly the damage has been done. The official generally knows when he has muffed one, and often the inclination is to even the score by calling one the same way on an opponent.

What do coaches want in an official?

(*1*) Complete honesty
(*2*) Deliberate and not flash calls
(*3*) Cooperation with the players instead of a policeman attitude
(*4*) Complete knowledge of the rules
(*5*) One hundred per cent effort to move around the court and get into position to call the plays. He shouldn't call anything he doesn't get a full look at.

In closing, it might be well to mention that a martyr complex in an official has become slightly nauseating.

Let's face it, coaching is tough and officiating is tough. If you can't take it, get out. Life is tough too. Some people even get out of that, and I'm sure that at times both coaches and officials, given a gun at the right moment, might be facing homicide charges in the morning. It's not enough for an official to say, when criticized, that he is honest. Blind men can also be honest.

RULES

As I've said at the beginning of this chapter, the two major weaknesses in the world's fastest growing sport are officiating and the advantage the excessively big or tall man has over the small man. Officials have to make many judgment calls, and judgment is a vague and fleeting thing in human beings. And nature produces size. We can't cut down tall boys like tall trees, nor do we want to. And, whether you believe it or not—most people do—a good big man beats a good little man in sports most of the time.

Because the pay-off is localized in a round hoop ten feet above the floor, basketball accents the advantage or the disadvantage—depending on how you look at it—of the seven-foot lad. I can see in the future a game played with Bill Russell of San Francisco (six foot, ten inches) funneling the ball into the basket at one end and Wilt "The Stilt" Chamberlain of Kansas (seven feet) doing the same thing at the other end. The game would be a travesty. We might as well call it funnel- or dunkball. It might be wise to have an assistant on each team throw the ball in the general direction of the basket and see whether Wilt or Bill can out-funnel each other.

Please don't take this as a criticism of these two fine boys. They are great specialists because of their excessive size. But what are we going to do about this situation? Here we have a physical advantage that eliminates maneuvering and finesse from the great game of basketball, which is primarily a game of balance and team play instead of four supporting cast members and one feature player.

There are a number of suggestions that will cut the big man down to size. Let's explore some of the ideas that might establish a balance between the big, nonmaneuverable man and the other men.

I look on basketball as a game more of balanced performers than of specialists. That, you must constantly keep in mind, is the essence of *incentive basketball*. I'm interested in preventing the game from becoming dunkball or funnelball. The game and the way it is played is all that interests me.

In recent years the foul lane has been widened to 12 feet in an effort by the rule-makers to cut down the effectiveness of the big man. This means, of course, that no offensive man can loiter in the foul lane area for longer than three seconds. This, in effect, forces the big man to move through the foul lane area. He can't sit in there. More than three seconds in the lane and it's a loss of the ball. This has served to open up the game partially.

But the big man still can rebound the ball and funnel it in the basket. Maybe by the time this book has been read the rule-makers will have seen fit to prohibit the offensive man from dunking the ball from above the basket. This would at least equalize the "permitted" skills of the defensive and offensive men who can leap above the hoops. It is a ridiculous situation when the offensive man is permitted to stuff the ball down into the basket but the defensive man is not permitted to "stuff it up," so to speak.

Another rule that might excite some thought is one that would forbid scoring on rebounds. In other words, the ball would have to be passed off after a shot has been taken. Kids play this type of game in school-yards and gyms all the time. They call it half-court. You can't shoot with a rebounded ball. It has to be thrown out to the side or back before another shot can be taken by the offensive team. This would be simple to enforce merely by taking the basket away and awarding the ball to the team in possession from an out-of-bounds offensive court position. Isn't it sufficient in itself that the big man gains possession of loose balls for his team merely by being tall?

Much publicity has been given to the professional rule requiring a shot every 24 seconds. The pros wanted to eliminate stalling. Some such rule might be invoked in the latter stages of college games, maybe in the last three minutes. Or it might be feasible to allow officials to invoke the rule any time during the game when they feel stalling tactics are being employed. We give officials enough other judgment calls. One more won't hurt anyone.

The professionals have made a run-and-shoot game out of their show, on the assumption that the customers like to see cheap baskets and scores soaring into the hundreds. I can't help but feel that this is a false premise. My mail and conversations with others seem to bear me out. Many people like to see some sort of control game, and any rule that serves to standardize types of offenses and defenses is robbing the game of one of its most interesting aspects: teams with varying styles of offensive and defensive play.

No one wants to see the same type of anything too often, whether it be football, baseball, tennis, or basketball. The average fan wants variety, which, after all, is still the spice of life. The happy basketball fan must be the one who sees a tournament with such teams as the Oklahoma Aggies, St. Louis, Kentucky, LaSalle, Duquesne, San Francisco, Indiana, and Utah. All these teams have varying personalities in the form of different patterns of offensive and defensive play. Compulsory time shooting would almost wipe that out of existence.

As for the one- and two-shot foul rule, I'll dismiss any discussion of that with the comment that good teams shoot their fouls and poor ones don't. John Bunn, a member of the rules committee, put it beautifully when he said to complaining coaches, who had lost because their teams were outshot from the foul line, "Teach your boys not to foul so much." Sometimes you win with that rule and sometimes you lose. There is some wailing that too much time is spent going to the foul line. Yet these same people never say a word about the numerous huddles, time-outs, and substitutions in football, or about the delay and stalling around in baseball games. Maybe we need even more loafing and stalling around in this mad game, until the fans and some coaches and officials get caught up with what is really going on.

☆ 13

PROFESSIONAL
BASKETBALL

Some nine years ago I was preparing a dude ranch in Wyoming for the summer season, when I received a long-distance call from St. Louis. "Would I like to coach the St. Louis entry in a new professional basketball league?" the caller asked. I swam a horse across a turbulent river, hitched a ride forty miles to the nearest airport, and the next morning arrived in St. Louis ready for I knew not what.

I was met by the owners of the new team and the gentlemen of the press. All were enthusiastic about the prospects for the new league. "Here," they said, "is something comparable to the big leagues in baseball. We have wealthy men with big arenas and auditoriums. It will simply be a matter of time for this idea to grow bigger and bigger."

I felt the same way but unfortunately things haven't quite worked out that way. It now appears that the only thing that can save professional basketball, as we know it today, is television.

What has happened to this wonderful dream? What has caused professional basketball teams to fold in cities that should be able and willing to support them? Why do some of the teams still in the pro league have to play home games in isolated cities and towns miles from their actual home bases? Why can't professional basketball flourish?

There are a number of things that may have caused this condition. I'll attempt to enumerate some of them as they appear to me. A newspaper man from Pittsburgh told me at the time the defunct Basketball Association of America was being organized that the trouble with the league was its lack of real financial backing. He said there were not enough men in the picture who were willing to lose money for years in order to build the sport—men with the kind of money big league baseball people have, men with the kind of money they could afford to lose when they didn't win their division or the league championship. "Everyone in your league *has* to win to stay in business, and professional basketball will fail because the right kind of venture capital isn't behind it," he told me. Maybe he was right. Time alone will tell. But it is only fair to mention that several of the owners have taken terrific beatings and still are coming back for more.

The fast pace of the modern game of basketball, especially of the professional game, makes the life of a player comparatively short, so a career in the sport isn't likely. The players try to get the top dollar for their services while the getting is good. In order, therefore, for the owners to meet the payroll, games are played almost every night during the season with travel in between. This means the players become exhausted, which naturally slows down the game. Once speed is missing from the game of basketball it has lost one of its dominant features. I once read a newspaper comment about an impending pro basketball game to the effect that the game should be worth watching since each team had managed to get a night's rest.

Recent rule changes in the pro game haven't helped to make it more attractive, although I'm sure the owners and coaches feel it has. The rules as now constituted tend to streamline the teams so that all look alike and play alike, now that George Mikan has retired. The necessity to shoot for the basket every 24 seconds has killed the maneuvering technique. The rule against zoning has handicapped teams with lesser material and reduced the possibility of planned defenses and more than occasional upsets.

Coaches in the pro league no longer are teachers and coaches, but are cheer leaders and substitutors playing hunches. They have no time to plan defenses and offensive changes, even if they are technically competent to do so. When I was with St. Louis we won many games by using motion pictures of our opponents that disclosed weaknesses. We made specific adjustments during practice sessions to take advantage of those inherent weaknesses. I wonder how much the pro football coach could prepare for a game if he had to play every day. This is not an effort to be critical of the coaching, but merely to reiterate that too many games have to be played in order to stay out of the red.

The theory that grouping the finest players together should bring about the finest basketball is a beautiful one. However, it breaks down in another way. Salary increases for pro players, so the players tell me, go to the scorers. So, on some occasions, especially in the last few weeks of the season, the players start *shooting* for next year's contract. I doubt that, but it could happen; and the NBA is a shooter's league, not a defensive league.

Then too you hear stories about player salary jealousy in the pro league. One coach once said that he would like to have the perfectly balanced financial team: all $5,000 players. He said that when the salaries vary too much you have a situation in which the $3,000 player won't pass to the $9,000 player, especially when the $3,000 player thinks he's as good a performer anyway. You don't have that trouble if the top salaried man is a Mikan or a Fulks, someone who can lead the team into the play-offs and extra money.

What then is the future of pro basketball, if any? (And I sincerely hope it lives and flourishes.) The pro game furnishes an additional incentive for graduating college players. They can acquire a nest egg for the future. It also furnishes fine entertainment for thousands. I like to watch the pros when they are really rested. The quick answer might be the one my Pittsburgh friend offered: more men with real dough that they can afford to write off if they lose, so that fewer games have to be scheduled. Then there would be time for real coaching of planned defense and offense, a real chance for resting, and a return of speed to the game.

Let the teams tour the hinterlands during the exhibition season. But once the regular league play gets underway, schedule games about two or three times a week at the most, and really go. Less playing would give coaches the opportunity to teach different defenses and offenses. It would provide more time for the advertising build-up of each game. These are a few of the ideas that are being batted about. I'm sure the owners have thought of them.

Going back to something I mentioned at the beginning of this chapter, I'd like to say just a word about television. TV can be the salvation of the pros. It can provide necessary money to help offset losses at the gate and it can bring the game of basketball into the living rooms of people who perhaps have never seen a basketball game. Properly controlled, TV can do a big job for pro basketball. Television and televising owners might be able to save pro basketball. Let's all hope so. Then that fabulous organization, the Harlem Globetrotters, who pack the house wherever they go, can continue on their merry way carrying basketball to all parts of the world, without stopping to play doubleheaders with some of the pro have-nots to help get them out of the red. Pro basketball should be able to color its own books or cease to exist.

★ 14

TO THE HIGH
SCHOOL COACH

"Just as the twig is bent the tree's inclined," Alexander Pope said, and, if a boy gets off on the wrong foot in junior and senior high school, he well can be handicapped for the remainder of his athletic career. The secondary school coach has a grave responsibility. He teaches a boy when he is most impressionable, before the youngster has formed definite opinions.

I suppose the real start on right fundamentals begins in junior high, since most boys start to play basketball at that stage of their lives. Someone has said that the real coaching is done in the secondary schools. By that they mean the high schools and junior highs. I'll go along with it. I've known many high school coaches who were much better coaches than their college counterparts, but the college men got by because they were great recruiters and had more facilities at their command.

It should be fairly obvious that the coaching approaches in high school, college, and professional basketball are and must be different. The eager approach to the game of most high school coaches is demonstrated by their attendance at coaching clinics, which has largely been responsible for the growth in basketball techniques and for the steady flow of good material to the colleges. Some high school coaches, however, may be faced with another problem: whether to win games or to do what is best for the overall athletic development of the boy.

If the high school coach is fortunate enough to have a six-foot, four-inch boy he is undoubtedly forced to play him in the pivot area, for the simple reason that he needs him on the boards to retrieve the ball for his smaller men. In playing the big man in the pivot area, the coach isn't helping the boy's overall court proficiency. Therefore, most college coaches, looking at high school material, are sometimes not really able to evaluate the high school player. You can't get a real line on the boy if he's in a zone on defense and inside on offense.

If the high school coach is willing to suffer the slings and arrows of reporters and spectators by playing the boy outside part of the time where he can learn to maneuver and by allowing him to play man for man on defense, he'll be doing the boy a favor. The youngster will develop into a better basketball player. If the coach does this and as a result isn't winning, he'll take an awful roasting from the uninformed fans—or should I say the unsympathetic fans?

I am asked constantly to give certain fundamental drills and warm-ups for high school practices. These generally are of value to the beginner, but I have found from observation and other sources that the best way to learn basketball is in the quarter-court scrimmage with the ball changing hands between the offense and defense after each basket.

Although this is probably old stuff to many high school coaches, I will repeat here for those starting out in the coaching field a few of the rules that may be consistent with the later collegiate development of the boys' technique.

(1) Shooting is first, with eye-high set shots and driving off the fake sets dominant. Then come the various jump shots.

(2) Encourage a minimum of dribbling.

(3) Have the boys front (face) the basket at all times.

(4) Teach the one-hand bounce pass through congestion to moving pivot men.

(5) Encourage shooting outside from no greater than a 17-foot radius of the basket.

As far as I am concerned, these are basically sound rules that boys will carry with them through their entire basketball careers—high school, college, or professional.

Just as a big boy should be permitted to develop

evenly all over the court, so should the boy who is never going to be big concentrate on outside set shooting. The world is filled with six-foot basketball players— small by college and professional standards—who will be zoned by big men when they drive in to the basket. And they'll rarely get the shot to the basket against good big men. So, if you're a six footer and can't count on being any bigger, practice those twenty-foot one-hand and two-hand set shots. The hardest thing in the world is to tell a boy who has been a fine, well-rounded basketball player on a championship high school team that he is too small for college ball. But with the widening of the foul lane there promises to be an increase in the use of the zone defense, which will accent set shooting more than ever before.

Too much cannot be said of the real influence the right kind of a high school coach can have on the boy who is in the formative years of his life. The high school coach can help the boy by stressing the importance of a high scholastic standing derived from good study habits. Boys in high school are more eager to play than at any other time in their life, for they have discovered for the first time that they are somebody as far as the community is concerned. Therefore they can be molded more easily. The coach in high school can do more of this than can any college coach or teacher. In the summer many high school coaches supervise playgrounds, where most youngsters are introduced to the fundamentals of basketball and other sports. This serves the dual purpose of keeping the boys off the streets and of affording an opportunity for the coaches to ground the boys properly in fundamentals.

One word of caution: don't give your team complicated patterns of attack. High school boys generally aren't ready to handle complex systems of offense and defense. If five boys did nothing but give and go (pass off laterally and drive directly for the basket) and keep properly spread out, they would play a pretty good game of basketball. Naturally, you alone know how advanced a pattern they can absorb. But don't overburden them so as to rob them of their individual good points. These still have a place in properly balanced pattern basketball.

MEMOIRS OF A
SUPERFLUOUS
COACH

SOMEONE HAS SAID THAT THERE ARE TWO KINDS of coaches: those who have been fired and those who will be fired. I repeated that remark once to a West Coast writer, who immediately took me up on it. How true that was, he agreed, for Amos Alonzo Stagg, grand old man of football, had just left the College of the Pacific after a famed career as a fine coach. The writer remarked, "Yes, no future in it. But, oh, what a past—some 66 years of it for Stagg."

To some I may sound cynical. I'd rather think I'm a realist. What should be a noble profession, the genuine influencing of young men toward the goal of living a life of sportsmanship in a needy world, has become a ratrace to oblivion—a vicious cycle of wins and, if you fail to win enough, the sack. I've never been fired, but I have had enough fine coaching friends who have. To me there can be only one sensible goal for competitive sports: fair field, no favorite, and may the best team win after it has been trained and schooled in the best techniques possible by the teacher-coach.

What has brought about this situation in which no one wants to coach, but merely to rest on the tenure of teaching? I suppose many things. What has brought about the attitude of certain faculties toward members of the coaching profession? At many universities the coaches are not named in the faculty directory. Yet, at one time, William Lyon Phelps of Yale said, "Gentlemen, you are the real teachers. You meet the boys when they are at their emotional heights and at their emotional depths. You are with them more often than their other professors and you should know them better. And you, consequently, can be a greater source for good than their scholastic professors."

What has happened to that idea?

Who is it that said, "When the feeling to exercise comes over me I lie down until the feeling leaves"? Many and varied are the attitudes of people in and out of the sports world toward athletics generally and toward athletic competition specifically.

My first eye-opening shock came early in my coaching career. I was at a small college in western Pennsylvania. My team managed to defeat a great

Long Island University team on its own floor, after LIU had been undefeated at home for seven years. This notable win was followed by a success over a fine City College of New York five, 50–27. I was called to the president's office sometime later and expected at least a few words of approval for a team performance that had caught the attention of the sports world. Imagine my surprise and disappointment when the kindly president properly deflated me. He didn't even mention the victories. He said to me, "Ken, I understand several of your basketball players sleep occasionally in psychology class. I'm afraid you're working them too hard."

Being a brash young man, I mentioned that I had heard others than athletes were often known to sleep in the same class. Maybe I should have folded my coaching mantle then and there, but I went on to live and learn.

The professional sports field graveyard is filled with businessmen who have been highly successful in private business, only to fail miserably in the professional sports business for many reasons. One is that businessmen never quite realize that athletes, often good ones, are artists who can't be handled with the same degree of disregard with which they might handle their foremen or day laborers.

One owner in the pro basketball league had a unique idea. After a successful season he hit upon the idea of mailing out contracts with from a $500 to a $1,000 cut in each contract. This, mind you, in the face of a gen-

erally acknowledged successful season. This plan included the contract of a star player. When questioned
about the good judgment of such a scheme and about the
effect on the moral of the squad, the millionaire owner
said, "Well, I expect they'll all want raises and I think
I've put myself in a better bargaining position by making
the first move."

One year later, as the team sat in the dressing room
with an even better season behind it and playing for the
championship, the owner came to the dressing room and
said, "I have made up a poetic couplet, boys: Give me
more than ever before." One tall Western realist, who
remembered the cut the year before, said with a murder-
ous twinkle in his eye, "Mr. X, charity begins at home."
I don't know when I've laughed louder.

Since then the pro league has had many and varied
experiences. Many of the original members have fallen
by the wayside. This recalls an incident involving
Maurice Podoloff, president of the league. A St. Louis
sportswriter queried Mr. Podoloff as to why several of
the famous Illinois whiz kids had been allocated to the
Chicago Stags, particularly Andy Phillip, who lived
near St. Louis and quite obviously would have been a
great attraction for the Bombers. Podoloff honestly
pointed up the question with the following answer:
"You cannot have a big league in most sports unless you
have a successful entry in both New York and Chicago."

Since that time, Chicago has been without an entry.
Who knows, maybe the sports world would do well

even without New York? The basketball league, if
Podoloff's statement is to be taken literally, is no longer
big league. Or maybe his statement will call for a
little adjustment. A suggestion has been made that
the famous Globetrotters be entered as a unit, a suggestion within the realm of possibility. However, they
seem to be doing pretty well on their own. And, since
the purpose of professional sports is to make money,
maybe they would lose some of their world-wide glam-
our and do worse.

Someone has said that uneasy lies the head that
wears the crown, and I think the hardest person in the
world to teach is a favorite. If you win, so what. If
you don't, you're a bum. This experience inspired
the following doggerel, fatalistic as it may sound.

I'm an ordinary figure in the field of athletics,
Where the wind blown out by coaches is an
    insult to phonetics.
As the children of the trackmen have the big-
    gest kind of thighs,
And the child of Betty Grable has that some-
    thing in her eyes,
My position in the bottom of society I owe
To the qualities bequeathed me by my parents
    long ago.
My father was a halfback and, until he broke
    his hand,
Was the best old backer-upper that ever strode
    the land.

My mother was a swimmer and dad's promises
        believed,
And they thought of great successes for the
        son they had conceived.
Since that time I've lived by coaching,
Not much money, not much fame,
Lots of worry, second guessing,
Lots of hurry, lots of blame,
But my mother and my father are the ones
        who gave me name.
Yes, you've guessed it, I'm an outcast,
And t'will always be the same.
Win or lose, you're still a dummy,
You can't beat the coaching game.

Several summers ago I went to Puerto Rico to coach
a team. There are not many tall boys in Puerto Rico,
so the teams were matched fairly even. But there was
one boy who was six feet, five inches tall. He was a
valuable threat on the backboard to the smaller manned
teams. Two teams argued over his services and the
feud became a cause célèbre that went almost to the
supreme court of the island. The newspapers daily
were filled with the debate. It was heartening to see
such enthusiasm and interest in sports again. How
different than in one city where a nationally famous and
supposedly civic-minded group invited the national
championship basketball team to a luncheon in the team's
honor and asked the boys to pay for their lunch.

I have gone to Europe for the armed forces and have been inspired by the interest of our soldiers in the athletic picture back home. Sports is one thing that distinguishes this country from so many others. The State Department has tried the idea of getting sporting America across to foreign countries to combat communistic influences among the labor groups, which are largely the sports-minded groups abroad. I have also been fortunate in being selected to take a trip through South and Central America and to Japan, where we discussed coaching techniques and told our soldiers about their athletic heroes at home.

I heard this story in Bad Tolz, where Hitler's Panzer divisions formerly trained. It seemed Herr Wagner believed that he was a mouse and went to a psychiatrist to see if he could rid himself of this obsession. After some time and effort on the part of the doctor, he was pronounced cured. "You may go now," said the doctor. "And, Herr Wagner, remember you are a man and no longer a mouse."

Herr Wagner left the hospital, walked down the street, and then suddenly rushed back to the doctor. "Herr Doktor," he cried, "there is a large cat down the street!"

The doctor replied, "Remember, Herr Wagner, you no longer are a mouse, but a man."

"Ja," said Herr Wagner, "you know that and I know that, but does the cat know it?"

Yes, we know that basketball is a wonderful sport,

and now the whole world is getting to know it. Maybe coexistence will ultimately come about through international sports games. Sports for sports sake, where boys and men can train and compete and lose and laugh, and have memoirs when they too become superfluous. These coaching years have been a series of rewarding experiences in meeting many wonderful friends and some enemies.

And so my respects to all coaches and teachers, in and out of the profession, wherever they are or may have been:

> Isn't it strange
> That princes and kings,
> And clowns that caper
> In sawdust rings,
> And common people
> Like you and me
> Are builders for eternity?
>
> Each is given a bag of tools,
> A shapeless mass,
> A book of rules;
> And each must make,
> Ere life has flown,
> A stumbling-block
> Or a stepping-stone.*

---

* "A Bag of Tools," by R. L. Sharpe, has appeared in *Masterpieces of Religious Verse*, James Dalton Morrison. ed.. Harper & Brothers, New York, 1948.